Reading Beowulf

The first page of Beowulf, *in manuscript British Library Cotton Vitellius A.15, folio 132r (olim 129). Courtesy of the British Library.*

READING
BEOWULF

*An Introduction to the Poem,
Its Background, and Its Style*

By

J. D. A. Ogilvy

and

Donald C. Baker

Drawings by Keith Baker

University of
Oklahoma Press
Norman and London

BY J. D. A. OGILVY

Books Known to Anglo-Latin Writers from Aldhelm to Alcuin, 670–804 (Cambridge, Mass., 1936)
Books Known to the English, 597–1066 (Cambridge, Mass., 1967)
The Place of Wearmouth and Jarrow in Western Cultural History (Jarrow Lecture, Cambridge, Mass., 1968)
(With Donald C. Baker) *Reading Beowulf* (Norman, 1983)

BY DONALD C. BAKER

(Ed.) *The Late Medieval Religious Plays of Bodleian MSS Digby 133 and e Museo 160* (Oxford, 1982)
(With J. D. A. Ogilvy) *Reading Beowulf* (Norman, 1983)
(Ed.) The Manciple's Tale, vol. 2, part 10 in *A Variorum Edition of the Works of Geoffrey Chaucer* (Norman, 1984)

Library of Congress Cataloging in Publication Data

Ogilvy, J. D. A. (Jack David Angus), 1903–
 Reading Beowulf.

 Bibliography: p. 197
 Includes index.
 1. Beowulf. I. Baker, Donald C. II. Title.
PR1585.O37 1983 829'.3 83-47835
ISBN: 0–8061–2019–3

To Bertram Colgrave
Scholar and Friend

Contents

Illustrations

Preface

THE past thirty years have seen an enormous surge of critical interest in *Beowulf.* Its prominence today is the more remarkable because its language is incomprehensible to most readers, its verse forms strange and confusing, its diction formulaic and repetitive, and its moral and ethical assumptions rather foreign to those popular in our own day. For all that, teachers of literature surveys who present *Beowulf* in a modern translation are nearly unanimous in their opinion that it is one of the few poems in the course that can be counted upon to arouse a real and enthusiastic response from the student.

Its attraction lies partly, we think, in the poet's steady, uncompromising narrative of the exploits of a hero who is vastly greater than most men but not a superman like Achilles; a man who has enormous power and authority and uses them only in the service of his people and his friends; and a man who has great self-respect befitting his achievements but is not given to the maudlin egocentrism and self-pity that occasionally overcome other epic heroes. He is human in that he is capable of being defeated, not by trick or guile but in what for Beowulf is fair combat with a supernatural creature. He is the distilled essence of the northern European heroic literature, devoid of those weaknesses of character that one sometimes encounters in sagas. The Christianity of the poem is almost as important a part as the heroic code that Beowulf follows. It is the Christianity of the Dark

Ages, as heroic in its own way as the code of the Germanic civilization to which it was grafted. Beowulf does steadily what is right, for himself and for others. He does not engage in wars of conquest but defends his own land, with the result that, unlike a typical Germanic warrior-king, he brings peace to his people in his own time. God lends his power to aid Beowulf, but only when Beowulf has the strength to use that aid. In spite of the fact that Beowulf engages supernatural foes—a troll, a troll wife, and a fire-breathing dragon —there are no miracles to save him. Beowulf is under no illusions. Life is hard, but it is worth the struggle. *Beowulf*'s poet is at least as able to see life steadily, and see it whole as are some of Matthew Arnold's favorite poets.

The poem is popular not only because of the story but also because of the skill of the poet. Writing in a heavily formulaic style, with a traditional diction and verse, the *Beowulf* poet has a command of variety, comparison, and contrast; a sense of proportion; a sense of when repetition is effective and when it is not. He knows when to describe fully and when to leave the scene to the reader's imagination. He knows how to handle Germanic understatement as few other poets have done. Not many passages in English literature have the total effect of the last three lines of *Beowulf* (3180-82), which suddenly leave to one side the heroic achievements of the prince of warriors, and conclude by going directly to the rather simple heart of the man:

> cwædon þæt he wære wyruldcyninga
> manna mildust ond mondwærust,
> leodum liðost ond lofgeornost.

(They [the mourners after Beowulf's death] said that he was, of all worldly kings, the mildest of men, the gentlest, the kindest to his people, and most eager for fame.)

In the pages that follow, we have provided a modest introduction to the reading of the poem that assumes that the reader is keen on learning about *Beowulf.* We present first a survey of the few facts about the poem: the unique manuscript in which it is found, its history, and the probable circumstances of the poem's composition; the historical background that provided the materials for the *Beowulf* story; and something of the way in which the poet has put together the stories, along with their parallels and allusions. We are concerned primarily with *Beowulf* as a poem and with the skill of the poet in framing his materials, using them to foreshadow and reflect each other. We have offered a rather large consideration of the versification of the poem—large because numerous conflicting theories may reduce the beginner to utter confusion on matters considerably less vital to the appreciation of the poem than the scholarly sound and fury surrounding them might imply: The reader need not fear, however, if he has any knowledge of prosody. A chapter has been devoted to the style of the poet, his use of formulaic diction, and the effect of the Anglo-Saxon language itself upon the poetry. And we have devoted a chapter to describing the critical response of our age to *Beowulf.* The select bibliography is rather large because we have made an effort not necessarily to select the very best studies for the attention of the student but to give a representative sampling of important work done from the many different approaches to the problems of the poem. Although we have very definite ideas about the poem, we have made every attempt to avoid dogmatism and to allow other views a proper expression. We have not been able, alas, to restrain ourselves from comment on obvious absurdities.

Although we occasionally allude to the language of the poem—for example, to Anglo-Saxon poetic vocabulary and to Anglo-Saxon sentence structure in relation to versification—we refer only in passing to technical linguistics, such as dialectal forms and dating on linguistic evidence. Studies in these fields are complicated and, we believe, inconclusive. The student interested in such matters might begin with the section on language in Frederick Klaeber's third edition (1950), but he might be wise to wait until he has completed at least a year or two of Anglo-Saxon before he devotes much time to the subject.

All of our quotations from *Beowulf* are from the most useful of editions, that of Klaeber. The translations are our own. We have tried to keep the notes to a minimum, limiting them to documentation that is too cumbersome for the text and to an occasional excursus that has no place in the chapter.

Because we cannot date Anglo-Saxon poems accurately and because some poems that may have served as links in a chain of influence have been lost, there is little point in speculating on the influence of one Anglo-Saxon poem on another. Some scholars believe that *Andreas* was influenced by *Beowulf*—that Saint Andrew is presented there as a Christian hero in contrast to the warrior Beowulf. There is nothing impossible in this view, but not all scholars accept it.

During the centuries that Anglo-Saxon poetry lay forgotten in libraries, it could exert no influence; but even since its rediscovery its direct influence on other literature has been slight. Some episodes and characters in J. R. Tolkien's *Lord of the Rings* are based on *Beowulf*—for example, the court scene, in which Fork-Tongue is obviously Unferth; and John C. Gardner's *Grendel,* a sort of parody of the events at Heorot, has been rather popular. On the whole, however, modern authors have recognized and avoided the difficulty of re-creating the tone and manner of a poem so different from the literature of our own time.

On the other hand, *Beowulf* has been enormously influential in shaping our view of Anglo-Saxon life. Because of its inclusion, even if only in part and in translation, in so many English courses, it is the most widely known document of the Anglo-Saxon period. About 1900 there were even illustrated children's *Beowulf*s, but they seem to have gone out of fashion. Among scholars more widely acquainted with the period, only *The Anglo-Saxon Chronicle* and the Venerable Bede's *Ecclesiastical History* can match its influence. Like Bede's work, *Beowulf* presents an idealized picture, and the two are largely responsible for the romantic regard in which the nineteenth century held what Tennyson called "Teutonic father ages." One negative way of judging this effect is to compare the distinctly earthy characters of Gregory of Tours's *History of the Franks* with the characters in Bede and *Beowulf*. J. S. P. Tatlock had this point in mind when he asked in a lecture, "What would have happened to our views if Bede had written the *History of the Franks* and Gregory had composed the *Ecclesiastical History?*"

The contrast between *Beowulf* and *Roland* is less marked; but *Roland* is a poem of defeat resulting from hubris (Old French *desmesure*) and the treachery of Ganelon. Beowulf, whether or not he suffered from *hubris,* was victorious in death because of the loyalty of Wiglaf.

Compared to the actual conditions of Anglo-Saxon life, *Beowulf* is rather unrealistic; but in our age, in which literature often goes out of its way to be sordid, a statement of the ideal may come as a relief. Certainly *Beowulf* expresses one of the dominant ideas of English legend—the theme of Jack, the Giant Killer and Saint George and the dragon: if one is brave enough to challenge the monster, he may win. Alfred wandering alone through the marshes of Somerset but still determined to save his kingdom from the Danes; the companion piece of Robert Bruce and the spider; the half-mad Sir Richard Grenville sailing the little *Revenge* into the midst of the huge Spanish fleet—none of them exactly sober history—all belong to this type. In the nineteenth century the Spartans at Thermopylae and, thanks to Macaulay, Horatius at the Bridge, were adopted as part of this folklore. So was *Beowulf.*

Today it is rather unfashionable to speak of national character, but that does not mean that it does not exist. The folklore of a culture not only expresses this character but reenforces it and, to some extent, forms it. No one can prove that English folklore had an important part in leading England to challenge, and eventually to defeat, the dangerous and aggressive empires of modern history from that of Philip II to Hitler's Third Reich. On the other hand, such behavior by a people who did not believe that even the most ferocious monster must be fought and can be beaten would be surprising. Whatever the influence of this belief, *Beowulf* is an expression of it.

Acknowledgments

AS are all other students of *Beowulf,* we are indebted to the thorough and sane edition of the poem by Frederick Klaeber, and especially to his voluminous notes; likewise, to Raymond W. Chambers's monumental *Beowulf: An Introduction,* which is indispensable for its store of information of historical and folkloristic nature. We gratefully acknowledge permission from D. C. Heath and Company to quote from Klaeber's third edition of 1950, which is the source of all quotations from the poem, including the emendations of Klaeber marked by brackets. We also acknowledge permission from Columbia University Press for the quotations from *Elene* and other Old English poems as edited in their *Anglo-Saxon Poetic Records.* Macrons have been eliminated from quotations for simplicity's sake.

We also wish to express our gratitude to the Trustees of the British Museum for permission to publish the photograph of a leaf of MS Cotton Vitellius A.15 and to adapt as drawings their photographs of items in the Sutton Hoo treasure. And, of course, we express our thanks to Keith Baker for doing the drawings. Donald C. Baker also wishes to thank the Council on Research and Creative Work of the University of Colorado for a faculty fellowship that gave him time to do the research for his part of the book.

J. D. A. OGILVY
Boulder, Colorado

DONALD C. BAKER
Boulder, Colorado

Reading Beowulf

Chronology of *Beowulf*

Since the date and place of the composition of *Beowulf* are uncertain, a precise chronology is impossible. All dates are A.D.

521   The death of Hygelac is entered in Frankish annals.

597   The Gregorian mission reaches England; the conversion of Kent. These events ultimately result in the conversion of all England and the introduction of writing of more than brief runic inscriptions.

660-700   The approximate floruit of Caedmon, according to Bede the first English Christian poet. The writing down of his verse by the scholars of Whitby is the first recorded writing of Old English poetry.

700-850   The most probable approximate date for the composition of *Beowulf.*

1000   The approximate date of the extant manuscript of *Beowulf* (Vitellius A.15).

1563   The *Beowulf* manuscript is in the hands of Laurence Nowell, whence it passes into the hands of Sir Robert Cotton (1571-1631).

Ante 1677   Franciscus Junius (1589-1677) transcribes section 5 of the poem (Bodleian MS Junius 105).

1700   The Cottonian Library, including Vitellius A.15, is deeded to the nation.

1705   H. Wanley *(Librorum . . . catalogus)* transcribes the incipits and explicits of Vitellius A.15.

1731   The manuscript is damaged in a fire in Ashburnham House.

1787   The Thorkelin Transcripts are made.

1815   G. J. Thorkelin produces the first printed text of *Beowulf.*

CHAPTER 1

The Manuscript

L IKE every other important Old English poem, *Beowulf* survives in a single manuscript. In fact, almost the entire corpus of Old English poetry as we know it today is contained in only four manuscripts: the Exeter Book (Exeter Cathedral Library, MS 3501), the Vercelli Codex (Vercelli, Biblioteca Capitolare 117), MS Junius 11 (Bodleian Library, Oxford University), and British Library Cotton Vitellius A.15.[1] All four manuscripts date from approximately 1000 A.D.

Cotton Vitellius A.15, which contains *Beowulf,* is a composite volume. The first 93 folios, sometimes called the Southwick Codex, were not bound with the remainder (folios 94-209) until early in the Renaissance, probably by Sir Robert Cotton's bookbinder, a notorious misbinder and cropper of manuscripts. The second part, the Nowell Codex, contains part of a legend of Saint Christopher in Old English; *The Marvels of the East,* also in Old English; an English translation of the spurious letter of Alexander to Aristotle; *Beowulf* (folios 132v-201v);[2] and a fragment of an Old English poem, *Judith.*

The Nowell Codex belonged in 1563 to Laurence Nowell, one of the curiosi who did so much to save early manuscripts

3

after the dissolution of the monasteries (an interlinear gloss by him appears on folio 9 of the Exeter Book). Later the manuscript came into the possession of Sir Robert Cotton. During the Civil Wars, Cotton's collection was stored at Stratton, Bedfordshire, and protected from the attentions of Puritan bookburners by the high sheriff, Bromfall of Blunham. In 1731, while stored at Ashburnham House, the collection was seriously damaged by fire, which destroyed about one hundred manuscripts and charred a good many more, including Vitellius A.15. The upper and outer edges of this manuscript were scorched and have been slowly crumbling ever since. Fortunately, two transcripts were made in 1787, when it was in better condition than it is today, one for and the other by G. J. Thorkelin. Before the fire H. Wanley had transcribed the incipits and explicits in 1705, and Franciscus Junius had transcribed one section (section 5) in full. This transcription is now Bodleian MS Junius 105. All these transcripts are helpful in reconstructing damaged sections of the text.

Eventually the Cottonian Collection came into the possession of the British Museum. Today each leaf of Vitellius A.15 is encased in transparent plastic to protect it from further harm. The manuscript has twice been reproduced in facsimile—first by the Early English Text Society in 1882 (Original Series no. 77), reproduced with new plates in 1959. The entire Nowell Codex appeared in 1963 as no. 12 of *Early English Texts in Facsimile,* which had earlier reproduced the Thorkelin Transcripts as no. 1 of its series. Of the accompanying texts the homily on Saint Christopher, *The Marvels of the East,* and the letter of Alexander were published by Stanley Rypins (Early English Text Society, Original Series no. 161 [1924]). *The Marvels of the East* was printed in facsimile by M. R. James for the Roxburghe Club (1929), and the text of *Judith* has been edited by, among

4

others, E. van K. Dobbie, in *Beowulf and Judith* (Anglo-Saxon Poetic Records, vol. 4 [1954]).

The Nowell Codex was written by two scribes, one of whom (S1) copied the first part of *Beowulf,* and the other (S2), the second. Therefore, obviously, all the items of the codex must have come from the same library, though they were not necessarily bound together immediately after copying. Nothing is known of the history of the manuscript before it came into Nowell's possession, but from the number of pages missing from the beginning of *Judith,* we might suspect that it was not originally bound with *Beowulf,* for the greatest losses of folios usually occurred at the beginning or end of a manuscript. Kemp Malone considers that *Judith* was bound with the rest of the codex in Nowell's time or a little earlier. The first four selections, however, seem to be a compilation of writings on monsters and marvels, which may have been put together by the compiler of this manuscript or may already have been assembled in its exemplar. Early legends of Saint Christopher report that he was a *cynecephalos*—a dog-headed giant: *healfhundisce man* in Old English—and he is so depicted in manuscript illustrations. *The Marvels of the East* contains, among other things, "the anthropophagi and men whose heads do grow beneath their shoulders" and a visit to the gate of hell by Mambres the magician (one of Pharaoh's sorcerers who originally appeared in an Old Testament apocryphon); the pseudo-Alexander would be a fitting companion piece to Munchausen. The assembly of four such works in one volume can hardly have been accidental.

On the whole, the manuscript text of *Beowulf* is remarkably good. It is reasonably complete, whereas considerable portions of many Old English poems have been lost. More than half of *Judith* has disappeared; *Maldon* is defective at both beginning and end; *The Fight at Finnsburg* is a mere fragment printed from a single folio, now lost; the conclusion of *Daniel* has been lost; and a number of folios, probably eleven, are missing from *Genesis* and *Exodus*. For *Beowulf*, on the other hand, we have a text complete at beginning and end and with no obvious lacunae of any considerable length. Although there are many words and short passages about which editors are less than certain, no reasonably competent scholar of Old English has any trouble following the story as a whole, and most of the text is fairly straightforward reading.

Difficulties with the text arise from three causes: scribal error, defects in the manuscript, and our own ignorance. The Vitellius text was copied by West Saxon scribes but rests—immediately or ultimately—on an Anglian original. We have no way of knowing how many copyings occurred between the original manuscript of the poem and the Vitellius text. There may have been only one, or there may have been three or four. Even a single copying would be enough to produce a considerable number of errors. In a good scriptorium, a text considered important (for example, the Bible or a work of Augustine) would be carefully proofread and emended, but there is no evidence of such proofreading of *Beowulf*. The scribes of *Beowulf* were competent workmen, but there are some obvious errors in the text (for example, the *he* for *ne*, which makes nonsense of line 1130). Certain other passages (for example, lines 168–69) are so difficult to interpret that we are tempted to assume that a line or more has been lost.

Damage to the manuscript varies from the loss of a letter or two that can be replaced by a fairly certain conjecture (as in lines 15 and 21) to the almost completely lost passage in lines 2227–31, by far the worst-damaged part of the text.

It is easy enough to distinguish damage to the manuscript

from possible scribal error, but what we take for scribal error may be the result of our own ignorance. Like other Old English works *Beowulf* contains a considerable number of words that seldom or never recur in other Old English writings and for which we have no Latin gloss—our commonest source of information on the meaning of Old English words. *Icge* (line 1107), used to describe the gold laid on the funeral pyre of Hnaef, is such a word. It may have been a perfectly good Old English word, easily intelligible to the author and his audience, or it may be a scribal error that a contemporary of the poet would have had no trouble in correcting, but we moderns are puzzled by it. Besides our difficulties with vocabulary, we are often troubled by the poet's habit of compressed and allusive asides. In lines 168-69, referred to above, we cannot be sure whether our difficulty results from our ignorance of Old English habits of thought and expression, from our uncertainty about the possible meanings of *gifstol* and *myne wisse*, or from scribal error.

Nevertheless, as we have said, considering the condition of Old English manuscripts in general, we have a remarkably good text of *Beowulf.*

CHAPTER 2

Beowulf and Other
Early Germanic Poetry

THE author of *Beowulf* was well acquainted with the body of Continental legend that underlies most Anglo-Saxon secular narrative poetry. Occasionally a poem deals with a contemporary event. The two most important examples are *The Battle of Brunanburh,* which commemorates the crushing defeat of a coalition of Scots and Vikings by Aethelstan in 937, and *The Battle of Maldon* (often called *Byrtnoth's Tod* [*The Death of Byrtnoth*] by German scholars), about the defeat of an English force by Vikings in 991. Otherwise, secular poems largely deal with Continental material, which almost certainly reached Britain as oral tradition, though the history of *Genesis B* (see below) shows that transmission by manuscript was not impossible. Sometimes *Beowulf* itself is the only evidence for the presence of a tradition in England; sometimes there may be the evidence of a fragment of manuscript, and one use in *Beowulf* is reinforced by a letter of Alcuin (735–804), the Northumbrian scholar who went to France to head the palace school of Charlemagne and later to become abbot of Tours. Alcuin's letter is one of the few contemporary references to Anglo-Saxon poetry. The earliest, and the most valuable, is that of the Venerable Bede in his *Ecclesiastical History* (731), book 4, chapter 24, to the poet Caedmon's metrical paraphrases of Scripture (ca.

670), probably the first Anglo-Saxon Christian poetry to be written down. At one time the poems in MS Bodleian Junius 11 at Oxford, whose contents somewhat resemble the works attributed to Caedmon by Bede, were considered the work of Caedmon and were referred to as the Caedmonian Poems. *Genesis A, Exodus, Daniel,* and *Christ and Satan* might conceivably be by Caedmon; but *Genesis B,* an Anglo-Saxon adaptation of a Continental poem on the fall of Satan, could hardly be his work, and none of the poems is very seriously attributed to Caedmon today.

Asser (d. 909) the Welsh scholar whom Alfred the Great (849-899) summoned to assist in the restoration of learning in England, and who wrote a life of Alfred, discusses Alfred's taste for Anglo-Saxon poetry but unfortunately gives no titles. William of Malmesbury, a twelfth-century historian who apparently had access to sources that have since been lost, also discusses Alfred's poetic tastes, as well as the poetic skill of Aldhelm (640?-709), the first Englishman to compose much Latin verse that has survived. His English verse has not. According to William, Aldhelm's congregation was inclined to idle in the market square instead of coming to church. Aldhelm lured them into church by beginning a poem in front of the church and then going inside to coax them in after him. So excellent was his verse that they all followed. This *carmen de triviis* (song of the crossroads), William says, was still sung in Malmesbury in his own day.

Alcuin bitterly rebuked Higbald, abbot of Lindisfarne, for allowing the song of Ingeld, prince of the Heathobards, to be sung in his monastery. Alcuin's letter (ca. 800) reinforces allusions to Ingeld in *Beowulf,* lines 2020-69, and *Widsith* (a hodgepodge of notes on the rulers of Continental Germanic tribes, probably a scop's catalogue of his repertory), lines 45-46.

The tale of the death of the Frisian Finn at the hands of

the Danes (*Beowulf,* lines 1066-1169) is supported by a fragment, a single leaf of *The Fight at Finnsburg* (see Klaeber's edition of *Beowulf*). The allusions to other traditions (e.g., that of the Volsungs, *Beowulf,* lines 874-97) are not supported by other English evidence but no doubt rest on traditional tales.

Besides the poems on Old Testament material—*Genesis (A* and *B), Exodus, Daniel,* and *Judith* (the last preserved in the same manuscript as *Beowulf*), we have a number of poems on New Testament material, mostly apocryphal. Four of these —*Elene* (the discovery of the True Cross), the *Fates of the Apostles, Juliana* (a saint's life), and *Christ* are signed by the runes for Cynulf or Cynewulf woven into the closing lines. Some scholars have attributed poems of similar style but unsigned to Cynewulf or classified them as "Cynewulfian," belonging to the school of Cynewulf. Since Cynewulf was a fairly common name and we have no idea which Cynewulf signed the poems, the attribution is not very useful.

At first glance it might seem that the composition of religious poetry would call for different techniques from those of the writing of heroic poetry, but it did not. For example, it used many of the same formulas (see the opening formulas in chapter 9), and the subject matter called for similar vocabulary, for example, the decapitation of Holofernes by Judith and of Grendel by Beowulf. Andrew's adventures among the Marmadoneans, who ate nothing but human flesh and drank only human blood, are quite as spectacular as the events in *Beowulf.*

Efforts to relate *Beowulf* to Anglo-Saxon religious poetry either in date or in content have proved unconvincing, but the religious poems do give us a standard of sorts by which to judge *Beowulf.* We do not, however, have much in the way of secular poetry with which to compare the poem. We do not even know how much has been lost.

One consequence of our uncertainty of what constituted the corpus of Old English secular poetry is that we have no way of judging *Beowulf* in its contemporary context. It is as if we had only one full-length Elizabethan drama and only very sketchy information about the Elizabethan stage. Was *Beowulf* only one of a number of poems of the same kind? Was it the best of these poems? Did it rest on an earlier poem on the same subject? We cannot be sure.

At one time it was rather widely believed that *Beowulf* was the lone survivor of a considerable number of poems of the same kind, and scholars were inclined to bewail the carelessness and indifference of those who had allowed these priceless literary treasures to be lost. A salutary caution against too uncritical an acceptance of this view can be found in Kenneth Sisam's *Studies in the History of Old English Literature.* Many Old English poems have undoubtedly been lost, but on the surviving evidence it seems probable that most of them were epic lays—poems of 300 to 1000 lines dealing with a single episode, for example, *Finnsburg, Maldon,* and *Brunanburh.* These lays were probably of two kinds: those dealing with contemporary events, like *Maldon* and *Brunanburh,* and those dealing with legendary material, like the fragmentary *Finnsburg* and *Waldere.* Quite possibly there were cycles of such lays—strung together, perhaps, with sagalike narrative—dealing with certain legendary figures or series of events such as the feud between the Danes and the Heathobards; but we have no evidence of poems of the scope of *Beowulf.*

Since secular poetry was usually recited to a group for an afternoon or evening's entertainment, as is the lay of Finnsburg in *Beowulf,* a poem of a few hundred lines was more suitable for this purpose than one of several thousand. Even in composed religious poetry, most works were relatively short. *Judith,* we may conjecture, was approximately 800 lines; *Christ and Satan* was 732; and the *Phoenix,* 677. *Elene* contains 1320 lines; and *Andreas,* 1722, or, if we include *The Fates of the Apostles,* 1844, Perhaps each of the latter was broken up into two or three readings. *Genesis (A* and *B)* and *Exodus,* considered as wholes, are rather long, but they are more collections of epic lays *(The Offering of Isaac, The Crossing of the Red Sea)* than coherent poems.[1]

Besides being a good deal longer than an epic lay (3182 lines), *Beowulf* differs in method. Instead of dealing with a single event, it presents three main episodes in the life of the hero spread out over more than fifty years. This difference may result from the influence of the classic epic or of Christian Latin poetry. Whether other Old English poems like *Beowulf* existed but have been lost is anyone's guess, but if they did exist, they have disappeared, and it is not impossible that *Beowulf* was unique. Certainly it is unique among surviving Old English poems.

Beowulf is unique not only in scope and method but also in subject matter. Old Norse literature deals with gods who are sometimes all too human in their behavior, and with men who are also extremely human in the pejorative sense; that is, they play almost exclusively for their own hand and are activated for the most part by the baser passions—notably greed, hatred, and vengefulness. Much the same may be said of other early Germanic literature. The story of the *Niebelungenlied* is scarcely edifying; those of Heremod (briefly alluded to in *Beowulf,* lines 901-13 and 1709-22) and *Finnsburg* are, as far as we can judge from the remaining evidence, no better.

In *Beowulf,* on the other hand, we encounter a selfless hero—almost, but not quite, a demigod—though we may, if we wish, assume a demigod in the pre-Christian form of the story. But in the story as we have it, we encounter a mortal hero of incredible strength and valor who employs these qualities primarily for the good of his hereditary friend, Hrothgar (who had sheltered his father in exile), for the good of his prince, and for the good of his people. Not only do we have no other poem that presents such a hero; we have no allusions to such a story.

CHAPTER 3

Date and Authorship

A T one time scholars believed that they could accurately date Old English poems on the basis of linguistic forms and the use of poetic formulas.[1] *Judith* was A.D. 725, *Beowulf* 740, and so on. Today this rather touching faith has all but evaporated (for a commentary on the weaknesses of dating by linguistic forms, see Kenneth Sisam, *Studies in the History of Old English Literature*). A realization that poetic formulas were the common property of all Anglo-Saxon poets rather than phrases borrowed by one particular poet from another has destroyed our faith in their usefulness for dating or for discovering the relationship between two poems. The dating of the manuscript of *Beowulf* as about 1000 on paleographic evidence can be accepted with considerable confidence. Beyond that all is speculation. There are no allusions to the poem in the other literature of the period and nothing in the poem that relates it to any event in English history. The death of Hygelac in his Frisian raid (*Beowulf,* lines 1202-14, 2354-59), an actual historical occurrence, is dated about 521 in the Frankish annals and is alluded to in the *Liber de monstris et beluis (Liber monstrorum, Book of Monsters),* but this date is too early to be a particularly useful terminus a quo.

The Christian elements in *Beowulf* allow us to set our terminus a quo a little further ahead. The year 650 is about as early as we could reasonably expect to find such elements interpenetrating the materials of a secular poem, and even that date seems rather early. In attempting to narrow the date beyond 650-1000, we must recognize that we are resorting to speculation.

The picture in *Beowulf* of life in the heroic age seems more consistent with the turbulent ways of the Heptarchy than with the piping times of peace of Athelstan and his immediate successors. If we accept the opinion that *Beowulf* was originally an Anglian document, as almost all contemporary scholars do, a date after the outbreak of the First Viking Wars (ca. 870) seems improbable, for these wars swept away Anglian culture, except in one corner of Mercia (Worcester in the early tenth century would be a possible place of origin for *Beowulf,* but not a particularly probable one). Further, East Anglia and, particularly, Northumbria were slow to recover from the Viking ravages, and the recovery was soon interrupted by the events of the Second Viking Wars.

It seems likely that *Beowulf* was composed between 650 and 850, but we must remember that, at best, this is merely a statement of probability. In future scholars may discover— or think that they have discovered—ways to date and place the composition of *Beowulf* more closely. The proclamation of such discoveries should be greeted with interest but with a good deal of scholarly skepticism. Previous certainties on these points have not stood up well under critical scrutiny.

Examples of these lost certainties include the system of dating and interrelating Old English poetry referred to above and the dating and ascription of *The Dream of the Rood.* Fifty years ago most scholars ascribed this poem to Cynewulf or to the "School of Cynewulf" and dated it late eighth or early ninth century. Many equated Cynewulf with an eighth-century Northumbrian bishop of that name, and one German scholar even composed a book, *Cynewulf, Bischof und Dichter* (Cynewulf, Bishop and Poet). Cynewulf, or Cynulf, however, is a fairly common Old English name, and we have records of a number of other Cynewulfs—not to mention the probability that many more lived and died without leaving records. Consequently, attribution on the basis of name alone is a good deal less than conclusive.

To make matters worse, archaeologists now assign the Ruthwell Cross, on which an excerpt from the *Dream* is inscribed, to the later seventh century and do so with a good deal of confidence. If the archaeologists are right, we must either move Cynewulf and his school back by about a century or detach the *Dream* from that school and attribute it, as some earlier scholars did, to Caedmon or the Caedmonian school, for which the archaeological dating is about right. A really conservative scholar might be content to date the *Dream* as "probably late seventh century" and let it go at that.

Possible Places of Composition

If we accept the general opinion that the original dialect of *Beowulf* was Anglian, we merely narrow its place of origin to somewhere north of the Thames. It may have been composed in a monastery or by a member of the retinue of some bishop, but many feel that the author was more likely a courtly poet. The moral earnestness of the poem would not be out of place in a religious establishment, but its wholehearted acceptance of an essentially pagan warrior code appears more congruent with a courtly background.

If we wish to speculate further, three courts seem, at different times, to have offered suitable backgrounds for such a poem. The earliest is that of East Anglia in the middle and later seventh century. In that period East Anglia was a powerful, wealthy, and cultured kingdom. Its King Redwald (593-617) became hegemon *(bretwalda)* of all England south of the Humber and was strong enough to defy successfully Ethelfrith of Northumbria. Schools were established in East Anglia soon after its conversion, and the furnishings of the cenotaph of Sutton Hoo support the picture of the barbaric splendor of Germanic courts presented in *Beowulf.*[2]

Further, the artistic analogues to the jewelry of Sutton Hoo are Swedish. The Geats may have been ethnically and culturally indistinguishable from the Swedes, with whom they must have traded and intermarried in the intervals between wars.[3] In fact, the Wægmundings, the line to which Beowulf and Wiglaf belong (lines 2813-16), seem to have been as much Swedish as Geatish. After the disasters foretold in the last part of *Beowulf,* the remnants of the defeated Geats might naturally have fled to England. Wherever the poem was written, the concern shown by the author for the fate of the Geats might very well proceed from a special interest of the poet or his patron in the fate of his ancestors. The Swedish origin ascribed by some to the East Anglian royal house may really have been Geatish.

On the other hand, nationalism as we know it did not exist when the poem was written, and what might be called the sporting attitude of the poet accords a measure of respect and sympathy even to Grendel and his dam, who were at least good fighters despite certain regrettable defects of character (for a brief, beautiful comment on epic equity, see Simone Weil's great essay *The Iliad, or the Poem of Force,* pp. 32-33). The events narrated had occurred a long time ago, and even one of Swedish descent might feel a certain sympathy for the Geats, just as many nineteenth-century Englishmen whose ancestors had greeted the Stuart uprisings with indifference or hostility felt for the Stuarts and the

17

Young Pretender. One acquainted with Swedish legend would certainly have found the Geats playing a large part in it. Both Geatish and Swedish blood might easily have run in the veins of an English atheling. But the rather strongly pro-Geatish tone of the poem makes it probable that the author or his patron would regard himself as of Geatish rather than of Swedish descent.

One other point in East Anglian history may be used to lend some color to the ascription of *Beowulf* to that kingdom. The grim pessimism of the passage predicting disaster for the Geats may have matched the national mood of East Anglia after its crushing defeat by the Northumbrians at the Winwæd (655). To East Anglia this battle seems to have been what Flodden was to Scotland. After it the kings of East Anglia sank to the status of *subreguli* (tributary kings) of Northumbria or Mercia. For a people that had recently undergone such a disaster, the forebodings of the Geats would strike a familiar note.

To show the tenuousness of this sort of speculation, however, we should remember that Northumbria experienced a similar disaster at Nechtanesmere (685), where Ecgfrid and most of his host fell in a Pictish ambush. Northumbria recovered from this defeat better than East Anglia from the Winwæd, but it marked the end of Northumbrian expansion northwest and freed the Picts from Northumbrian overlordship. Bede gives the impression that Aldfrid, Ecgfrid's successor, faced the task of restoring a shaken and demoralized kingdom.

The court of Aldfrid (685-705) or of one of his successors, particularly that of Ceolwulf (729-37), to whom Bede dedicated his *Ecclesiastical History,* was one in which the author of *Beowulf* might have felt at home. Aldfrid the Wise, as the Irish called him, was a scholar, a bibliophile, and a poet. In his youth he had studied at Iona and elsewhere (his mother may have been a Scot). Some Gaelic poems attributed to him have survived; he is probably the Acircius who corresponded with Aldhelm and sent him samples of his Latin verse; and it would not be surprising if he wrote English verse as well. In fact, A. S. Cook suggested that he might be the author of *Beowulf*. This is an attractive speculation, and one wishes that there were some way of proving it. At any rate, the court of Aldfrid would have been hospitable to poets.

We have less information about Aldfrid's successors, but literacy was probably the rule rather than the exception among them, and it was also not uncommon among the noble Northumbrian laymen of this period. Lay youths were members of the episcopal schools of Aidan, Wilfrid, John of Hexham, and doubtless many others about whom we lack information, and these laymen apparently received about the same training as their oblate companions. In short, Northumbria must have produced an audience capable of appreciating *Beowulf* and may very well have produced a poet capable of writing it. One might almost say that Northumbria during its "flowering" was the logical place for *Beowulf* to appear. Whether it did actually appear there is another matter.

A third court in which *Beowulf* might have been written was that of Offa the Great of Mercia (759-96). From the correspondence of Alcuin with Offa and his circle it appears that Mercia was interested in learning. In one of his letters Alcuin recommends a student to Offa as a teacher. Very likely this student was intended as a member of a "palace school" like that of Charlemagne, whom some historians suspect Offa of imitating. If Offa had ordered the writing down of English poetry, he would have been paralleling or imitating Charlemagne, who, according to Einhard, his biographer, ordered the traditional Frankish poems to be written down.

19

As has been said above, English Mercia seems to have preserved more learning than any other part of England during the First Viking Wars. A poem written in Offa's court or an older Anglian poem preserved there might have survived in this area—for example, at Worcester, which preserved a considerable portion of our surviving English documents—and this poem might have passed thence into Saxon hands after the revival of Wessex under Alfred. For that matter, poetry may have been composed in English Mercia throughout the bad years of the Viking Wars, and *Beowulf* may be a part of that poetry.

So many interesting possibilities for a place of composition should warn us not to confuse speculation, no matter how scholarly, with certainty.

The Author of Beowulf

Students' beliefs about the authorship of *Beowulf* will naturally be colored by their theories of the composition of the early poems of any culture in general and the composition of Old English poetry in particular. During the past century various theories on these subjects have come into and—after a time—gone out of fashion. Most of the theories have contained a modicum of truth, though not necessarily a very large one. The composition of *Beowulf* will be discussed in greater detail below, but some general theories require discussion here.

The earliest of these is the belief that epics were concatenations of "tribal lays"—a theory that like the oral formulaic doctrine, was first applied to the Homeric poems and then spread to other literatures. The tribal-lay theory, like the doctrine of the communal authorship of ballads, had its greatest vogue in the latter half of the nineteenth century. A concomitant of the tribal-lay theory in Old English studies was that of multiple authorship, which was applied even to short poems, such as *Christ and Satan.* The pseudoscientific method employed was to count the terms for *God, warrior, sea,* and the like in the various sections of the poem and then note how many of the terms in section A did not appear in section B and vice versa. If, for example, section A contained 143 terms for *God* of which 39 did not appear in section B, and section B contained 132 such terms of which 44 did not appear in section A, and so on for the other items of the list, these variations were considered proof that sections A and B were by different authors. Perhaps the only comment needed on this method is that it produced a number of doctoral dissertations.

Some episodes and some digressions in *Beowulf* rather obviously rest on epic lays, but the application of the tribal-lay theory to the poem as a whole never aroused much enthusiasm. The essential unity of *Beowulf* is so obvious that scholars generally have flinched from the task of dismembering it. For one fairly recent attempt to divide *Beowulf,* that of F. P. Magoun, Jr., see chapter 10 below.

The theory of growth by accretion is somewhat more plausible—that is, the belief that someone composed a much simpler *Ur-Beowulf,* to which an undetermined number of later poets made additions until the poem reached its present form. A special subsection of this theory held that the original *Beowulf* was pagan but was reworked to incorporate Christian ideas.

So far as the growth of the story goes, accretion and progressive modification are certainly probable. The form in which the story reached the scop who gave the story its essential—and perhaps its final—shape is something we shall never know. If we did, we could give a definite answer to a very interesting question: How original was the author of

Beowulf? So far as the *poem* is concerned, the theory of growth by accretion has much less to recommend it.

The theory that a Christian veneer has been applied to an essentially pagan poem has been stated for other Old English poems besides *Beowulf*—notably *The Wanderer* and *The Seafarer.* Of late, for *Beowulf* this theory has gone out of fashion. An alternative opinion, particularly for *Beowulf,* is that the Christian veneer has been applied not to the poem but to the inherited pagan beliefs of the author—a statement that might be made about most professing Christians today. There is ample evidence that, for most Englishmen of the centuries after the conversion, the veneer was thin and patchy.

The most recent theory of the composition of Old English poetry—the (oral) formulaic—will be discussed in more detail below. Obviously it contains a good deal of truth, but certain of its offshoots are open to question. The idea that there was no such thing as a received text of an orally transmitted poem—that in each presentation of a story the author reclothed the outline of the tale in oral formulas—should be regarded with considerable skepticism. Considering the abundant evidence of the magnificent memories of the unlettered, the accurate oral transmission of a poem as long as *Beowulf* is not impossible. For example, part of the training of the Irish *filid* and *baird* consisted in learning a very large number of classic tales.[4] Although we consider improbable the oral transmission of *Beowulf* as we know it for some time before it was written down, it cannot be ruled out as impossible.

The following discussion rests on the belief that *Beowulf* is in the main, if not entirely, the work of a single author. From a poem—particularly a good poem—it is legitimate to assume a poet.

Unfortunately, what we can assume about the poet is extremely limited. First, he was a poet of very considerable abilities, expert in poetic technique and thoroughly acquainted with the conventional poetic themes and with the large body of Continental legend that constituted the chief part of the stock in trade of an English scop. Second, he was an earnest and idealistic soul, a poet of piety in the Virgilian sense and of *virtus* that shades into, but is not lost in, Christian virtue. Finally, he was no mere singer of the village square and the alehouse. He was as much a poet of the aristocratic way of life as the *trouvère,* though he sang of, and to, a very different aristocracy. It is true that singers of the fairs and alehouses—for example, the authors of *Horn* and *Havelok*—attempted to impart an aristocratic coloring to their tales. But, as Chaucer indicates in *Sir Thopas,* their aristocracy rings as false as a lead shilling. The author of *Beowulf* was to the manner born.

Unless we assume a Christian retoucher of the basic work, the author of *Beowulf* must have been a Christian, but we cannot be sure whether he was a layman or a cleric. In the Anglo-Saxon period almost anyone could compose poetry. Churchmen were no exception. Bede composed his death song in English, and two of Alcuin's Latin poems alliterate according to the English pattern. William of Malmesbury said that an English poem by Aldhelm was still sung in Malmesbury in the twelfth century. Moreover, William, who wrote as if he were acquainted with a collection of English poetry that had belonged to Alfred the Great, stated that Alfred considered Aldhelm the best of the English poets.

Some straitlaced clerics might, no doubt, have objected to a secular poem on pagan antiquity. As mentioned earlier, Alcuin was furious when he learned that the lay of Ingeld was being recited at Lindisfarne, but obviously the congregation of Lindisfarne did not share his views. Bede, writing about 730, complains that some bishops prefer a retinue made up of parasites and entertainers to the companionship of the godly; and Lul, writing a couple of decades later, implies that such entertainers—doubtless including poets—were present at banquets attended, and quite likely given, by clerics. *Beowulf* may have been composed in some clerical group of liberal views. Considering the way in which a military tone appears in much Christian poetry (for example, in *Judith*) and considering the high moral tone of *Beowulf,* a good many clerics might have considered the poem edifying. The *Aeneid* was highly thought of throughout the Middle Ages (though there were dissenters), yet Aeneas is, on balance, a less admirable character than Beowulf.

The rather common assumption that the author of *Beowulf* was literate is often thought to imply that the author was a cleric; but although evidence for lay learning (like evidence on almost any other matter in this period) is spotty, what we have does not justify the belief that learning was a monopoly of the church. A good many Northumbrian princes had been trained in Iona or elsewhere in Gaelic territory. Oswald had spent enough time among the Scots to learn their language, and Oswy, according to Bede, had been "trained and baptized" among the Scots. Oswy's son Alchfrid had been trained under Wilfrid and had learned enough of theology and church discipline to be a strong advocate of the Roman rite at Whitby (664). The scholarly tastes of Aldfrid of Northumbria have been discussed above.

It seems that in the middle of the seventh century a visit to Ireland was, for young Northumbrians, the equivalent of the eighteenth-century grand tour. In this connection, Bede's remarks in chapter 27 of book 3 of his *Ecclesiastical History* are informative:

> In this time many of the race of the English of both noble and humble birth, leaving their native island, traveled thither [to Ireland] for theological study or for a life of greater aus

24

terity. Some immediately undertook the monastic life; others preferred to go from the cell of one master to that of another to pursue their studies. The Scots [Gaels] gladly received all of them, fed and housed them without charge, and freely provided them with books and instruction.

Obviously most of these scholars were destined for the church, but there were exceptions. Also, instruction in non-theological subjects was possible. Aldfrid, for example, had learned how to compose poetry in both Gaelic and Latin. It is unfortunate that we know nothing about Oswald and Oswy except that they had learned Gaelic.

Another possible source of occasional lay education were the Scotti *peregrini*—the wandering Gaels—who turned up all over western Europe in the early Middle Ages. Wherever they appeared, they set up in business as schoolmasters. An anecdote of the time recounts that several of them arrived in France with a group of merchants. The merchants, as soon as they got ashore, began to hawk their wares. Not to be outdone, the Scotti began to cry: "Learning to sell! Who'll buy? Who'll buy?"

Such a wandering Scot was the first teacher of Aldhelm, and Dunstan in his youth was taught by others who had set up cells at Glastonbury. The Irish monks who played such a large part in the conversion of Northumbria and Mercia may also have set up schools. Not all who began their studies in Ireland, with the *peregrini,* or in the episcopal schools referred to above would learn much or, even if they planned to enter the church, persevere until they were ordained. Probably the proportion of lay to cleric among educated men was rather low, but one educated layman, if he was the right one, would be enough to compose *Beowulf.*

The aristocratic tone of *Beowulf* proves little or nothing about the calling of its author. Many abbots and bishops were men of high birth. Benedict Biscop and his kinsman Bede were apparently members of the royal house of Lindsey (a line only of *subreguli*—minor kings—it is true, but one that traced its descent some generations beyond Woden). Several archbishops of York were members of the royal house of Northumbria, and bishops, ex officio, ranked with secular princes. Also, clerics were attached to royal households as chaplains and secretaries.

In fact, there are so many possible walks of life for the author of *Beowulf* that it is idle to try to guess which he actually followed. All we really know is that he was a poet—and a good one.

CHAPTER 4

The Anglo-Saxon View

ALTHOUGH essential human nature probably has changed very little since the eighth century, many conventional beliefs have been altered. Poetic standards have changed with the shift from a preliterate to a literate society, and views of life and death have been altered by the introduction of Christianity. We seem to be inclined to think that the conversion changed Anglo-Saxons immediately from pagans into modern Christians. What really happened was rather different. Anglo-Saxons added Christianity to the heroic code. *Beowulf* is a product of this blending of old and new.

To the modern reader parts of *Beowulf* may seem unnecessary or needlessly long: for example, the many speeches, the digressions—or, as Byron calls them, "episodes"—and the repeated accounts of the fight with Grendel. To the author and, presumably, to his audience, however, these things probably seemed desirable embellishments. Fashions in narrative change. As late as the eighteenth century long, intrusive tales with practically no connection with the main story were considered legitimate additions to novels. Few of the digressions in *Beowulf* are nearly as irrelevant, and none is anything like as long. The two songs by scops in Heorot have no very clear connection with the story, but the allusions to Sigemund and Heremod are introduced in praise of Beowulf

27

or in advice about his future conduct. The speeches were part of the epic tradition and doubtless interested a poet and an audience concerned with courtly behavior. Repeated passages on the same subject are to some extent incremental: they never merely repeat what has been told before. Whether or not we admire them, we should recognize that they are part of the poet's method, not the results of ineptitude.

Nor should we blame the poet for our difficulties in following some of his allusions—particularly to the Swedish wars. Like the poet, his audience must have known a good deal about these events, so that allusions to Ingeld or Onela were as plain to them as allusions to George Washington or George III would be to us. The poet, after all, was not writing for our ignorant generation; he wrote for his contemporaries, as every author does.

We should also recognize that the poet is capable of artistic economy when it seems to him desirable. The two fights and the two gift givings at Heorot could easily have led to tedious repetition, but they do not. A bungler would have given us a chronicle of Beowulf's exploits between his visit to Hrothgar and the dragon fight. Our author plunges in medias res (for the second time) and takes care of as much of the interval as he considers proper in flashbacks. His sense of economy is also shown in the brisk way he treats the voyages to and from Denmark. The first takes about fifteen lines (lines 210-25); the second, about ten (lines 1903-13). Even the inclusion of the preparations for the voyages does not much more than double the length of the passages.

Inconsistencies in Beowulf

The digressive method of the poet and his habit of returning several times to the same material result in some apparent inconsistencies, though most of them can be explained away. The statement early in the poem (lines 202-204) that wise counselors encouraged Beowulf to undertake the adventure at Heorot may seem to conflict with Hygelac's statement (lines 1992-97) that he had tried to dissuade Beowulf, but that may merely mean that Hygelac and the elders of the court had not seen eye to eye on this point.

Beowulf's assertion that he will fight Grendel bare-handed so as not to take advantage of Grendel's ignorance of arms (lines 677-87) does not seem entirely consistent with the author's later statement (lines 2682-87) that swords were no help to Beowulf because his great strength always broke them, or with Beowulf's own regret that he can think of no way to fight the dragon without weapons (lines 2518-24). The discrepancy is not vast, but it does seem as if in the first passage Beowulf were making a virtue of his natural method of fighting.

In the Unferth episode (lines 499ff.) Unferth refers to doughty deeds performed by Beowulf before he came to Heorot, and Beowulf speaks of his swimming match with Breca as something he had done as a boy *(cnihtwesende)*. Elsewhere an allusion is made to Beowulf's achievements in youth (*on geoguðfeore*, line 2664). Yet in lines 2183–88 the poet tells us that for a long time the Geats had considered Beowulf rather worthless. This may be an inconsistency resulting from the poet's bringing in the ugly-duckling theme as an afterthought, but one might argue that there were two periods in the poet's youth—an early one (ages ten to sixteen?) in which he was slack and lazy and a later one in which he began to show his mettle.

In the descriptions of Grendel and the dragon the poet is not so much inconsistent as extremely vague, but we may doubt whether he visualized either of them clearly. The most specific information we are given about Grendel is that his head was a heavy burden for four men (lines 1635, 1640—two or three hundred pounds?). It seems doubtful whether a creature with a head this size or one that could carry a bag containing the bodies of twenty or thirty men could have got through the doors of Heorot. But then we do not know the dimensions of these doors. Our information about the dragon is even less specific. It had to rear up to seize Beowulf by the neck (lines 2688, 2692), and it was fifty feet long (line 3042). If we think of the dragon as a winged saurian (say, a crocodile), this seems out of proportion, but if we remember that the poet constantly refers to dragons as *wyrm* (worm, serpent), we may be able to visualize such a beast. Aerodynamically improbable as such a creature seems, the poet's dragon was a flying serpent, possibly with some stubby legs in front, of slight enough girth that Beowulf could cut it in two in the middle with his *seax,* whose blade was probably no more than two feet long. This idea of the dragon is not particularly dissimilar from that represented in illustrated manuscripts: a creature built close to the ground, with an inordinately long tail and a body of moderate size, no larger than that of a well-grown wild boar. Dragons in illustrations rarely look as if they would run to fifty feet overall, but very few heroes reached Beowulf's stature either. A single-handed attack on a dragon such as this would be a heroic but not necessarily reckless undertaking if one could guard against its fiery breath.

Even if we feel that the poet's description of his monsters is not very precise, he sins in good company. Anyone who attempts to picture the dragon in book 1 of *The Faerie Queene* is likely to end his days in a madhouse. This creature has a tail three furlongs (660 yards) long, yet we are asked to believe that it could be slain by the Red Cross Knight, who appears to be a man of normal size.

A minor inconsistency appears in lines 2291-94. Just after

the runaway serf has succeeded in stealing the cup from under the dragon's nose, the author, repeating a formula already used of Beowulf, remarks, "Thus may one not fated easily survive woe and exile, he who possesses the favor of the Lord" (lines 2291-93). It is true that the serf escapes the dragon, but when we next encounter him, he is *hæft hygegio-mor* (a sorrowful captive, line 2408) being forced to guide Beowulf's band to the dragon's lair. His good fortune has been, to put it mildly, rather brief. This anomaly is part of a larger inconsistency in the author's view of how far the Lord's favor can protect one from the troubles likely to result from disturbing a dragon's hoard.

Christianity in Beowulf

Most of the inconsistencies and apparent inconsistencies in *Beowulf* have to do with religion. For example, the Danes usually speak like Christians, as in lines 381b-82:

> Hine halig God
> for arstafum   us onsende,

(Holy God in his grace has sent him to us,)

Yet when he stopped to think of the matter, the author must have known that the Danes were pagans, as he has made them in lines 180b-83a:

> Metod hie ne cupon
> dæda Demend,   ne wiston hie Drihten God,
> ne hie huru heofena Helm   herian ne cupon,
> wuldres Waldend.

31

(They knew not God, the Judger of deeds, nor comprehended
the Lord God; nor indeed did they know how to praise the
Helm of the heavens, the Wielder of glory.)

This ignorance does not keep Hrothgar from delivering
what at first glance appears to be a good Christian homily
against pride and avarice (lines 1700-84). God, says Hrothgar, bestows wealth and power on some men, who, in their
folly, think that there can be no end to their good fortune.
Then they become proud and avaricious and end their lives
in solitary misfortune. The homily concludes with the commonplace that the miser has saved not for himself but for
an heir, who spends his wealth freely.

There is, however, one secular note. The wealth should
have been distributed to the miser's followers for fame (*on
gylp:* generosity was expected of a Germanic king). A thoroughly Christian homily (for example, Ælfric's homily on
Saint John)[1] would have demanded that the wealth be given
to the poor. In fact, in Ælfric's homily Saint John rebukes
the disciples of the philosopher Gratan for divesting themselves of their wealth out of mere vainglory (for *ydelum
gylpe*).

To both Hrothgar and the Christian homilist, vainglory
and avarice are sins, though for somewhat different reasons.
Therefore, their speeches sound very much alike. Hrothgar's
speech almost certainly shows the influence of Christian homi-
letic literature. Nevertheless, it is not a Christian homily; it
is *almost* Christian.

The same thing may be said of a great deal in *Beowulf,*
perhaps including the protagonist himself. But we must remember that it may also be said of a great many characters
and societies. The Christianity of every nominally Christian
society is contaminated by various non-Christian elements,
many of them inherited from its past. In Anglo-Saxon soci-

ety one of the principal contaminants was the warrior code, which was so deeply rooted that the church had to condone the blood feud down to the end of the Anglo-Saxon period.[2]

Yet to deny the name Christian to characters and societies affected by these contaminants, while it may be proper for the moralist, would be extremely confusing for the historian. It has certainly confused the discussion of the pagan elements in *Beowulf*. Unfortunately, the author has not given us a preface or a footnote on his hero's religion. It seems that when he stopped to think about it, he must have realized that Beowulf could not help being a pagan in the place and at the time in which he lived. Yet he makes Beowulf an admirable Christian except when Christianity and the warrior code conflict. Then Christianity comes off a poor second—as it did with most Anglo-Saxons.

Probably the author was not greatly worried by anachronisms, and certainly he was depicting the model secular hero—not composing a saint's life, an allegory, a homily, or (as some commentators seem to believe) a riddle. Therefore, he simply told his story and left us to worry about the side issues.

The principal "pagan" elements in the poems are Beowulf's funeral, the frequent allusions to *wyrd* (fate), and Beowulf's concern with worldly glory as a means to immortality.

There can be no doubt that Beowulf's cremation is a pagan rite. Unless *Beowulf* is a good deal older than most scholars believe, the funeral is a traditional archaism. The author may have found it in his sources for *Beowulf*. He certainly found it in such heroic poems as *Finnsburg*. The cremation was so firmly established in heroic literature that it passed on unchanged into the Christian period.[3]

On *wyrd* and earthly glory, however, *Beowulf* and Alfred's adaptation of Boethius show such close agreement that we can scarcely maintain that the views expressed by the Chris-

33

tian Alfred are pagan in *Beowulf.* One reason for considering the use of *wyrd* a sign of paganism is the antiquarian habits of many scholars who recognized the pagan origin of *wyrd* but did not consider how the use of the word might have changed. Perhaps we should remember that the newly converted English had only pagan terms—*frea, dryhten* (prince, lord, and thence God), *wyrd* (fate), and so on—for the expression of religious ideas. Once such a term was adapted to the statement of Christian ideas, it might very rapidly lose its pagan connotations.

Alfred the Great fitted *wyrd* into a Christian system. For him *wyrd* is the working of Divine Providence in temporary and transitory affairs (chap. 39, sec. 5, p. 128, lines 10-14):

> Ac ðæt ðætte we hataô Godes foreþonc . . . ærðæt hit gefremed weorðe . . . ; siððan hit fullfremed biô, þonne hataô we hit wyrd.[4]

> (But that which we call God's forethought . . . before it is performed . . . we call *wyrd* after it is fulfilled.)

Insofar as there is a distinction between Divine Providence and *wyrd,* it is that the former deals with matters eternal. It keeps the stars in their courses and brings around the seasons at their appointed times (cf. *Beowulf,* lines 1609-11, where God is spoken of as *Fæder* and *Metod*). *Wyrd,* though equally subject to God's foreknowledge, operates in affairs in which man's will is free.[5]

To one accustomed to the idea of immutable fate, the idea that *wyrd* is not completely inexorable is surprising. Yet both Alfred and Beowulf hold that *wyrd* may be influenced by human actions. According to Alfred, some things that God knows may happen, need not happen. As Payne points out (p. 49; quotation from chap. 41, sec. 3, p. 144, lines 16-20):

> Alfred separates events in time into two categories: the events that belong in one must happen; those in the other may happen or not.

> . . . ac sum hit sceal geweordˀan unanwendendlice; þæt bidˀ þætte ure nedþearf bidˀ, and his willa bidˀ. Ac hit is sum swa gerad þæt his nis nan nedþearf, and þeah ne deredˀ no þeah hit geweordˀed ne nan hearm ne bidˀ, þeah hit no ne geweordˀe.

> (. . . but a certain part must happen unchangeably; that is, whatever is our compelling necessity and His will. But a certain part is so determined that there is no compelling necessity of it, and even so does no harm if it come to pass; nor is there any harm even though it does not come to pass.)

As Payne sums up, "What God ordains must happen; what God merely knows can happen need not happen."

In this area of freedom *wyrd* has a choice: the power to slay and the power to spare. In this area man is free and may, within limits, bend *wyrd* to his will.

Rather surprisingly, Alfred says of this freedom (chap. 4, sec. 2, p. 142, lines 15-19):

> Ond men magon begitan þurh þone freodom swa hwæt swa hi willadˀ, buton deadˀ hi ne magon forcerran; æc hi hine magon mid goodum weorcum gelettan þæt he þe lator cymdˀ; ge furþum odˀ oreldo hie hine hwilum gelettap.

> (And through this freedom men can bring about whatever they desire, except that they cannot turn aside death; but they can delay it with good works, so that it comes later; indeed they can sometimes delay it until old age.)

This statement owes nothing to Boethius's *De consola-tione* 5, prose 3, with which it appears. In an extremely eventful life Alfred had seen apparently inevitable disaster turned aside by wisdom and resolution, and he speaks from experience.

Beowulf sometimes speaks as if he considers fate immuta-ble, as in the much-quoted "Gæd a wyrd swa hio scel!" (line 455). But he also says (lines 572b-73):

> Wyrd oft nered
> unfægne eorl,   ponne his ellen deah!

(*Wyrd* often spares an unfated warrior when his valor avails!)

"Fors fortes adjuvat." In lines 2291-93a the poet says:

> Swa mæg unfæge   eade gedigan
> wean ond wræcsid   se de Waldendes
> hyldo gehealdep!

(So may the unfated one easily survive woe and exile if he possesses the Ruler's favor!)

Note that in both passages the person whom *wyrd* spares is *unfæge;* that is, his case falls into Alfred's class 2. For the poet and presumably for other Anglo-Saxons, the idea of in-evitability resided more in *fæge* than in *wyrd.* If a man was *fæge,* not even *wyrd* could spare him.

It is easier to assume that the *Beowulf* poet, like Alfred, has fitted *wyrd* into the Christian system than to assume that he vacillates between the Christian and the pagan view when he alternately attributes the cause of an event to God and to *wyrd,* as when the outcome of Beowulf's struggle with Grendel is twice attributed to *wyrd* (lines 455, 734-36) and thrice to God (lines 438-41, 685-87, 705-707). If for him, as for Alfred, *wyrd* was merely the working out of the will of God, there was no inconsistency in the attributions.

Romantic commentators have seen in Beowulf "the brooding melancholy of pagan fatalism," or words to that effect. They forget that some centuries later a fatalistic and pessimistic form of Christianity (Calvinism) flourished not far from where *Beowulf* was written down. Neither Beowulf nor Alfred has much to say about the joys of heaven. The dying Beowulf, it is true, speaks as if he expects to stand before the throne of judgment (lines 2739b-42a):

> Ic ðæs ealles mæg
feorhbennum seoc   gefean habban;
forðam me witan ne ðearf   Waldend fira
morðorbealo maga,

(Mortally wounded, I rejoice in this: the Ruler of men shall have no occasion to accuse me of the murder of kinsmen,)

Nowhere in this speech, however, is there anything like the dying Byrtnoth's prayer for his own salvation in *Maldon.* Instead, Beowulf immediately turns his attention to the affairs of his kingdom. The poet does tell us (lines 2819-20):

> him of hræðre gewat
sawol secean   soðfæstra dom.

(His soul left his breast to seek the glory [or the judgment] of the righteous.)

Yet Beowulf seems more concerned with his earthly fame.

He bids Wiglaf have a barrow built near the sea so that his people and the passing seamen may call it Beowulf's barrow and remember him (lines 2802-2809). That is, he is concerned with the perpetuation of his earthly fame, as he was before his fight with Grendel's dam (lines 1386-89):

> Ure æghwylc sceal   ende gebidan
> worolde lifes;   wyrce se þe mote
> domes ær deaþe;   þæt biðʼdrihtguman
> unlifgendum   æfter selest.

(Each of us must experience the end of the life of this world. Let him who can achieve glory before death. That is best afterwards for the dead warrior.)

Alfred, in a passage entirely independent of Boethius, says essentially the same thing (chap. 17, p. 41, lines 3-6):

> Þæt is nu hradʼost to secganne, þæt ic wilnode weordʼfullice to libbanne þa hwile þe ic lifde, & æfter minum life þæm monnum to læfenne þe æfter me wæren min gemyndig on goodum weorcum.

(Chiefly, I desired to live nobly while I lived, and after my life to leave to the men who came after me the memory of my good works [or to leave the men who came after mindful of me for (my) good works].)

The syntax of this passage is difficult, but the sense is clear.

This is not the view of the ascetic Christian who despises earthly glory and fixes his eyes on the joys of heaven, but it is not exclusively pagan unless it ignores heaven and aims only at earthly fame. Alfred was a Christian whose thought was strongly influenced by the heroic tradition. So, it seems, was the author of *Beowulf.* The poet in his work and Alfred in his life embody the best of this combination. In terms of the time and place in which the poem was written, there is little inconsistency in its religious views.

CHAPTER 5

The Story: The Danish Adventures

THE central story of the poem is dictated by the author's purpose: to present an embodiment of the heroic ideal. In this presentation Beowulf's feats of strength and courage — remarkable as they are — are not the primary material. They are manifestations of nobility. The purpose is even more important than the deed. Every action is presented in the framework of *duguðe peaw* — the custom of warriors (line 359).

As a presentation of the ideal, Beowulf is a remarkably uncomplicated and straightforward character. Throughout the poem he never has a choice to make: the path of glory and duty lies so plain before him that he has only to follow it. A lesser man might vacillate between fighting Grendel or the dragon and keeping a whole skin, but Beowulf is not such a man. This is not to say that he is unaware of the possibilities of disaster. When he asks Hrothgar to allow him to await Grendel in Heorot, he observes with the grim humor of the fighting man that Hrothgar is not risking much. If Beowulf loses, Hrothgar will not have to feed him long. Indeed, he will not even have to bury him, for Grendel will leave nothing to bury. Before the fight with Grendel's dam Beowulf makes his will (an oral procedure among the Anglo-Saxons) and commends his retainers to Hrothgar's kindness.

Before the dragon fight he knows that, win or lose, this will be his last fight. But none of these considerations makes him think of abandoning his purpose.

In fighting, Beowulf has only one method: the frontal attack. He makes no special preparations for his first two fights, and for the third he takes only the minimal precaution of securing an iron shield—just enough to allow him to get home one good stroke on the dragon. This simple directness might easily have made Beowulf a "flat" character, a lay figure. That it does not is some measure of the poet's art. It is also justification for the long speeches in the poem. In them Beowulf emerges not only as a paragon of courtly behavior but also as an individual. To learn how he does so would require a more detailed analysis than is possible in a general introduction to the poem.

As has often been observed, the author centers his attention on Beowulf's encounters with monsters. Undoubtedly Beowulf had slain a good many men (we are told in passing that he killed Dæghrefn, the slayer of Hygelac, as he was in duty bound to do, but little is made of the episode). For a man of Beowulf's powers, killing another man was no test of knightly qualities. Only strife with monsters was a sufficient challenge to his heroism.

The poem falls into two parts. In the first part Beowulf appears as a daring adventurer and a loyal retainer (the episodes of Heorot). But even in going to Hrothgar's aid, Beowulf is no mere adventurer. The point that he does so not only for glory and gain but also as an act of hereditary friendship, because Hrothgar had befriended Beowulf's father and Beowulf himself, is not stressed, but for an Angle—particularly a Northumbrian—it would not have to be. Even modern Northumbrians treasure up an injury or a favor and wait with remorseless patience—even unto the third and fourth generations—to repay it. The second part shows Beowulf as king, though in the second part, too, we learn of his virtues as a retainer.

Summary

Lines 1–52. The story begins with Scyld Scefing, the legendary founder of the Danish royal line, and his descendants. As a child Scyld was cast ashore alone in a ship filled with treasure. He became a mighty king who freed the leaderless Danes from the persecution of their enemies. When he died, his body was laid in a treasure-laden ship and sent out to sea.

At first glance the opening of the poem with Scyld and the genealogy of the Danish kings may not seem the best way of beginning a poem about Beowulf, a Geatish hero. On consideration we see that it serves two purposes. It may be foreshadowing: the story of one who delivers a people in its hour of need. More important, it begins the poem on a high note. The story of Scyld suggests much more than it tells. The little boy who has come from an unknown land in a ship laden with treasure becomes the dead king sent by his sorrowing people in a ship laden with an equal treasure to a destination equally unknown (lines 40–47, 50–52):

> On his breast lay many an heirloom that must depart afar with him in the sea's power. No lesser gifts did they bestow upon him . . . than did they who in the beginning sent him forth, a child, alone over the ocean. . . . No man, no wise counselor, can truly say, no man under heaven, who received that cargo.

Is Scyld really dead, or is he "the king who was, the king

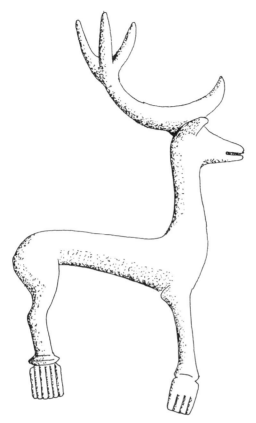

*The small stag found at Sutton Hoo, a mound in Essex that contained a seventh-century ship burial. It was almost certainly made to serve as the top of a standard ("segn") borne before a king. It is the sort of artifact that might have been placed in the burial ship of Scyld Scefing (*Beowulf, *line 47) or included as one of the mighty treasures given to Beowulf by Hrothgar. This and subsequent drawings by Keith Baker. Drawn after the original in the British Museum. Courtesy of the Trustees of the British Museum.*

who shall be"? The passage has the mysterious suggestiveness of the picture of the wounded Arthur borne to Avalon on a barge. For what it accomplishes, the passage is remarkably economical. It occupies only fifty-two lines.

Lines 53–193. After a little more genealogy come Hrothgar and the building of Heorot—a mighty king and a hall of unexampled magnificence. Whether there is a hint of hubris in Hrothgar's building of the hall is a matter of opinion. the poet does not commit himself. More important, the hall is held by a mighty war band, one that has reduced all the neighboring peoples to subjection. Yet this all-conquering king and his war band are powerless before the attacks of a mysterious creature and must suffer the humiliation of leaving their hall at sundown. The poet's remark (lines 138–40), "Then it was easy to find him who sought his rest farther off—a bed among the bowers," probably reflects the sardonic amusement of the subject peoples when they heard that their overlords could not hold their own hall.

This is a situation that calls for no ordinary hero, but a hero equal to the occasion is forthcoming. The opening passage about the Danes is not, after all, a circuitous approach but is the quickest way to plunging us in medias res. Most of what we need to know about Beowulf can be told after his arrival at Heorot.

Incidentally, in this passage we find the first manifestation of the poet's habit of alluding to events in the history of the Danes and the Geats that are completely outside the scope of the main story. Since the members of his audience were acquainted with the history of both peoples, they understood these allusions far better than we do and were much more aware of their significance. No sooner has the poet described the building of Heorot than he concludes (lines 82–85), "The building towered, high and horn-gabled; it awaited the battle

surges of the hostile flame" (the allusion is to the feud between Ingeld and Hrothgar, which led to the burning of
Heorot, which occurred after Beowulf's return from Denmark, the point at which the Danes drop completely out of
the story). The poet's concern with the fortunes of the Danish
royal house, and particularly with the good repute of Hrothgar, may merely reflect the importance of the Danes in early
legend, but perhaps the poet or his patron counted Hrothgar
among his ancestors.

Lines 194-228. Once the stage has been set, Beowulf is
brought to Denmark very expeditiously. Thirty-five lines suf-
fice to deal with his learning of the trouble in Denmark, his
decision to go to Hrothgar's assistance, his preparations for
the voyage, and the voyage itself.

When Beowulf reaches Denmark, the action is slowed to
a crawl by the demands of protocol: everyone must make
speeches. To the modern reader this protracted speechmak-
ing may seem dull. To the author, obviously, it was not.
Among later English authors only Jane Austen equals him in
her concern for the proprieties. In fact, *Beowulf* has sometimes been called the first English book of manners. Everything must be done in due form and order, and the most important part of that form was the speeches. Besides display-
ing courtly behavior, however, the speeches tell us a good
deal about the hero.

Lines 229-57. No sooner have Beowulf and his companions
disembarked than they are met by a detachment of the Danish
coast guard. The captain of the band addresses the Geats
with a judicious mixture of courtesy and firmness. First, he
states his office (produces his credentials, as it were) to establish his right to question them. The Geats, he continues,
have approached so openly that he is sure of their good in-

"The sea-wood on the shore,"its "twisted prow"topped by a carved beast. Such a ship is likely what was in the poet's mind: seventy to eighty feet long, powered by oars and a single sail. The Sutton Hoo ship bears no evidence of having been masted, but it almost certainly was. Beowulf's ship had a sail without doubt (line 1905). Details in the drawing above have been taken from the Sutton Hoo ship reconstruction and from eighth- and ninth-century Viking ships. Courtesy of the Trustees of the British Museum.

tentions; their leader is plainly a man of high rank. Nevertheless, he must know their errand. The blunt straightforwardness of his closing question is in amusing contrast to the diplomatic tone of the rest of the passage (perhaps he feels that the Geats have been a little slow to answer): "Now, ye far dwellers, ye sea rovers, hear my simple thought. Better be quick to tell me whence you have come."

Lines 258-370. Beowulf replies pacifically and states his errand (not for the last time). The guard promises to take care of his ship and guides him toward Heorot. Once in sight of Heorot, the guard turns back. Beowulf and his band approach the hall. At the hall they are accosted in courteous wise (*æfter æpelum,* line 332) by the majordomo. Beowulf requests an interview with Hrothgar, and the majordomo goes into the hall to report. All this is pure protocol. Its only possible use in the story is to build up gradually to the fight with Grendel and perhaps, by showing the discipline and morale of the Danes, to make the might of one who could ignore it more impressive. But the protocol itself doubtless had an interest for the audience. One can imagine them nodding their heads and murmuring, "Soð is. Swa sceal mon don" (That's right. That's the way it should be).

Lines 371-89. Hrothgar's reply to the majordomo is less formal than the preceding speeches but to us a good deal more informative. We learn that Beowulf's parents were Ecgtheow and a daughter of Hrethel, king of the Geats, and that Hrothgar had known Beowulf when he was a boy. We learn further that Beowulf's reputation for strength had already reached Hrothgar. From a later speech we learn that, by killing Heatholaf, a member of the powerful Wilfing tribe, Ecgtheow had begun a feud from whose consequences the Geats could not protect him and had fled to the court of Hrothgar. Hrothgar had received him and compounded the feud by paying the Wilfings an enormous *wergeld* (even that might not have been accepted if the Wilfings had not known that carrying on the feud would have involved them in war with Hrothgar). In gratitude Ecgtheow became Hrothgar's man: "He swore me oaths."

Lines 390-455. Beowulf is invited into the hall and enters with most of his troops but prudently leaves some to guard the spears and shields that have been stacked outside the hall (pirate captains, we are told, fired salutes to each other with shotted guns, and all these people were pirates). Once inside, he greets Hrothgar, identifies himself, gives his qualifications, and states his mission. In this speech he makes a testamentary disposition of his byrnie (coat of mail) if he should fall in battle and concludes with the fatalistic sentiment (line 455): "Gaeð a wyrd swa hio scel!" (Fate goes ever as it must). One more thoroughly steeped in Christian sentiments might have ended with, "And may God defend the right."

Lines 456–98. Hrothgar replies rather noncommittally. He observes that Beowulf's purpose is honorable, speaks of Beowulf's father, Ecgtheow, and goes on to tell of the sorrow and humiliation that he has suffered at Grendel's hands. This passage concludes with a rather grim picture of the fate of the Danes who, made valiant by beer, had from time to time stayed in the hall at night to challenge Grendel: "Then in the morning was this mead hall, this splendid hall, smeared with blood" (nothing else was left). This picture emphasizes the danger of Beowulf's undertaking and heightens the suspense.

Without specifically accepting Beowulf's offer, Hrothgar invites Beowulf and his companions to sit down to the banquet. Food and drink are served, and from time to time a scop entertains the company with songs.

Lines 499–528. In the midst of the feast Beowulf is challenged by Unferth, the *pyle* (see below) of Hrothgar, who sits at Hrothgar's feet. Unferth's speech and Beowulf's reply have aroused much scholarly speculation and debate. Before we consider them, let us look at the content of the passage:

Unferth is displeased with Beowulf's coming because "he would not grant that any other man should achieve greater deeds than he himself" (lines 503-505). He twits Beowulf with having undertaken a swimming match with Breca of the Brondings in a silly attempt to show off (*for dolgilpe*, line 509) and with having been beaten and adds that if Beowulf could not beat Breca, no matter what doughty deeds he had performed elsewhere, an encounter with Grendel would prove his undoing (note that Unferth gives Beowulf credit for military prowess, just as Beowulf, in his retort, admits Unferth's cleverness; whether these admissions show fair-mindedness or are the satirist's device of admitting an opponent's virtues only to make his faults look darker is a matter of opinion).

Lines 529-606. Beowulf replies by saying that Unferth has drunk too much beer and has the story wrong. The swimming match, he admits, was a bit of boyish bravado of which he is not particularly proud, but in it he not only outswam Breca but was dragged under by sea monsters *(nicors)* and escaped after a desperate struggle, in which he killed nine of them. He adds that he has never heard that either Breca or Unferth performed a comparable deed, though Unferth had brought about the death of his brothers and was noted for his intelligence. Further, says Beowulf, if Unferth were as good a man as he would like to think himself, Grendel would never have committed so many atrocities in Heorot. But Grendel has come to regard the Danes with contempt and does not expect them to fight back (this last remark indicates Beowulf's unflinching determination to fight Grendel despite Hrothgar's description of the fate of previous defenders of the hall and Unferth's warning; if he were to back out after making it, the Danes would never let him forget his boast). Then he reiterates his intention to challenge Grendel.

It would help us to understand this passage if we knew

precisely the meaning of the title *pyle,* applied to Unferth later in the poem. English glosses equate it with *rhetor, orator* (spokesman?) and, in compounds, *scurra.* Unfortunately, we have no very exact definition for *scurra* in the early Middle Ages. Sometimes it meant a mocker, sometimes a buffoon or other entertainer, such as a scop or gleeman. Unferth's position "at the feet of Hrothgar" is that assigned to the harper in the Old English poem *The Fates of Men.* With so many possibilities to choose from, we had better be guided by his actions, which combine those of a mocker with those of a special kind of spokesman—a devil's advocate, who taunts the guest to make him prove his bona fides. Since Hrothgar appears already to have accepted Beowulf, such a test seems somewhat out of place; but since, as the poet repeats in a later passage, Unferth was rather fuddled with beer, he may not have realized that his action was unnecessary. Or his jealousy of Beowulf may have made him officious.

Probably Unferth is expressing the feelings of the Danish warriors. For years they have been helpless before Grendel's attacks, and now a brash newcomer appears who is sure that he can succeed where they have failed. Doubtless they feel that he needs taking down a peg.

Looked at from another point of view, Unferth represents a type fairly common in early literatures—the mocker and belittler of the hero, the ungracious courtier: Loki in the *Eddas,* Sir Kay in the Arthurian legend, Euryalus at the court of Alcinous in the *Odyssey,* Thersites and Ajax in the *Iliad.* Except for a certain slow-wittedness, Ajax may be the closest parallel. He also is a man of valor, though not the equal of Achilles. We might regard Unferth as a Thersites who envies every valiant man if it were not for the respect with which Beowulf subsequently treats him, the esteem in which he is held in Hrothgar's court, and his possession of the sword Hrunting—obviously, from the poet's description, an heirloom sword of high quality. True, it failed against Grendel's dam, but any other sword forged by human hands would have done the same. Only an ancient sword, the work of giants, with magical runes on its hilt could prevail against her. No mere buffoon would have gained or kept possession of such a sword. According to Beowulf, Unferth had a considerable reputation. He seems to have been noted chiefly for cleverness, but he was very likely also one of the best surviving champions in Hrothgar's host. Because he was blamed for his brothers' deaths, his reputation had sinister overtones; but he was a man to reckon with.

The poet may have had several purposes in introducing the Unferth episode. If we had a number of long English secular poems, for example, complete texts of the *Waldere* (a fragmentary text in Klaeber's *Beowulf,* pages 266-68) and the story of Ingeld, we might find that such a passage was among the received poetic conventions of such narratives. Or if we had a full corpus of shorter works, we might find that some of them were early examples of the *conflictus,* the *débat,* or the flyting. Some Norse works are later examples of such a type; for example, the *Lokasenna,* in which Loki and the Aesir exchange insults. Just as the author introduced a bit of elegy into his poem, he may have decided to include a flyting.

To decide how the audience of Beowulf regarded this passage, we should consider how it seems to have affected the audience in Heorot. Hrothgar, who presumably could have cut Unferth short, allows him to proceed, and the other members of the court merely fall silent and listen, as they do to the lay of Finn, without expressing approval or disapproval. Possibly, like the audience at a modern gridiron banquet, they regarded the interchange as part of the afternoon's entertainment. Obviously the *pyle,* like the court jester at a later date, was allowed considerable latitude, and the butt of his ridicule was expected to reply in kind. Beowulf, in particular, is distinctly insulting both to Unferth and to the warriors of the Danes, yet no one seems to cherish any hard feelings. To a modern audience this debate may seem to go considerably beyond the bounds of good taste; but we should remember that the rules in such matters change. Apparently guests at Scandinavian feasts amused themselves by throwing picked bones at each other. In the *Waltharius,* a Latin translation of a Continental Germanic poem, the hero and his opponents, after lopping assorted limbs off each other, conclude a peace and sit down to a feast, during which they twit each other on the disabilities that their wounds impose. For example, Walter, who has lost an arm, is asked how he will embrace Hiltgund, the heroine. An audience accustomed to such robust humor might regard the exchange of compliments between Unferth and Beowulf as mere persiflage.

Whatever the conventions behind this passage, the poet makes good use of it in developing his story. From it we learn the hero's qualifications for cleansing Heorot. One who, as a boyish prank, could swim for seven days in full armor and dispose of nine sea monsters is just the man needed for the task. The speech also shows his resolution and overcomes any lingering doubts that Hrothgar may have had. Instead of rebuking anyone, Hrothgar rejoices that such a resolute champion has appeared.

Lines 607–41. The banquet continues. Wealhtheow, Hrothgar's queen, appears, does the honors of the hall, and thanks God that Beowulf has come to their aid (this is probably a bit of protocol that the audience would consider necessary). Beowulf replies suitably by reiterating his determination to overcome Grendel or die in the attempt. He speaks, we are told, *gud̄e gefysed* (ready for battle). The tension of the

fighting man before action is beginning to take hold of him—
a detail that would heighten the anticipation of an audience
of fighting men.

Lines 642–68. The feast continues, but soon it is time for
Hrothgar and the Danes to quit the hall. Hrothgar entrusts
the hall to Beowulf, exhorts him to valor, and promises great
rewards for success, *if he survives the conflict*—an observation that might have made a lesser man a trifle nervous and
one well calculated to heighten the anticipation of the audience. Then the Geats are left alone in Heorot.

Lines 669–96a. Beowulf takes off his armor, announces his
intention of fighting Grendel with his bare hands, since
Grendel does not know the use of weapons and using a
sword against him would be taking an unfair advantage, and
goes to bed. So do his men, but in a rather different state
of mind: "None of them thought that he would ever return
to his beloved homeland . . . where he had been reared, for
they had learned that a bloody death had already carried off
far too many of the Danes in that wine hall." The Danes at
the banquet had obviously let the Geats know that they considered them no better than dead men. But they were good
retainers. Honor bade them stay with their lord, and stay
with him they did, apparently without protest (like the companions of Ulysses, Beowulf's retainers are rather shadowy
figures; none of them says a word in the first section of the
poem).

Lines 696b–702a. Why, just when anticipation has been
keyed to its highest pitch, the author should tell his audience
that God would save the Geats through the strength of Beowulf is not clear. Perhaps the audience already knew the
outcome. At any rate, the stage is now set.

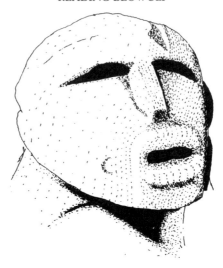

Although the inspiration for this drawing, a piece of sculpture found at the Lepenski Vir excavations in Yugoslavia, antedates Beowulf *by three thousand years, it would seem to be a representation of a water spirit or underground spirit not too far removed from the troll kind. It is not a "portrait" of Grendel but suggests (to us) the stony inevitability of the stalker of the moors. Courtesy of Thames and Hudson, publishers of the English version of Dragoslav Srejović's* New Discoveries at Lepenski Vir, *trans. L. F. Edwards (London, 1972).*

Lines 702b–19. Perhaps the author felt that anticipation is more effective than surprise. After noting the approach of Grendel ("In the dark night came stalking the walker in shadow"), he reminds us that Beowulf, fierce and resolute, awaits the outcome of a battle that Grendel is not destined to win.

The fight that follows is the high point not only of the poem but of Old English poetry. To be appreciated fully, it must be read in the original by one who has mastered the language. The description of Grendel's approach is interrupted briefly by the statement that never before had he found "harder fortune, fiercer hall thanes" (line 719). The Anglian character takes a grim pleasure in the anticipation of disaster. A later Northumbrian wrote in a lighter vein:

> "Ah Tam, ah Tam, thou'lt get thy fairin';
> In hell they'll roast thee like a herrin'.
> In vain thy Kate awaits thy comin';
> Kate soon will be a woefu' woman."

The anticipation in *Beowulf* is in a grimmer mood. At last Grendel is about to get what is coming to him, and there will be no "keystane o' the brig" to save him.

Lines 720–90. At a touch of Grendel's fingers the door, ironbound though it is, flies open, and he rejoices (somewhat prematurely, as we are reminded) at the rich feast spread before him. He seizes one of Beowulf's thanes and gobbles him up much as a wolf might eat a rabbit. Then he reaches out for another victim, and Beowulf grasps the clutching hand in his own. Pandemonium breaks loose in Heorot. Grendel struggles to get away but cannot, for his fingers are crushed in Beowulf's iron grip. The hall resounds, and the Danes in the married men's sleeping quarters are wakened by the uproar (but remain where they are). Mead benches are torn loose from the floor, and Heorot itself, though reinforced with iron bands, trembles to its foundations. Then comes a new sound, which makes the Danes cower in terror ("Weeping they heard, a lay of terror, God's adversary singing an unvictorious song").

Lines 791–836. In the midst of this tumult Beowulf's thanes draw their swords and try to aid their master, not knowing that Grendel cannot be harmed by weapons. As Grendel continues to try to pull away, a wound opens in his shoulder, both arm and shoulder are wrenched off, and he flees to his fen fastness mortally wounded. As a sign of victory Beowulf hangs Grendel's arm and shoulder under the roof of Heorot.

There has been much rather unfruitful debate on why Beowulf "allowed" Grendel to eat one of his companions before he grappled with him. We may say, if we like, that Beowulf subscribed to the theory that one must break eggs to make an omelette, that he needed a little time to gauge his opponent. If we wish to exculpate Beowulf, we may say that the sudden attack in the darkness of the hall gave him no time to save his thane. But perhaps we should recognize that, like the companions of Ulysses, Beowulf's thanes are expendable when their expenditure develops the narrative. The episode adds the crowning touch to the picture of Grendel's size, strength, and ferocity and would be cheap at the price of half a dozen thanes. No competent author would pause in the midst of this magnificent episode to explain why Beowulf would not or could not save his retainer.

Lines 837–915. A modern author might be content to stop here, but our author, like a Victorian novelist, likes a full denouement. In the morning the Danes follow Grendel's blood spoor to the mere and return rejoicing, racing their horses and singing Beowulf's praises. He is, they say, comparable to Sigemund, the great slayer of monsters and winner of glory, who killed a dragon and plundered its hoard, and Sigemund was the greatest adventurer since the unfortunate Heremod (Heremod appears in the West Saxon genealogy and that of the *Elder Edda* between Scyld and Scef). He was a great warrior, but was driven into exile for reasons not very clearly stated, but probably because he became harsh with his own people, in contrast to Beowulf, who of all mankind was "fairest to his friends." Both Sigemund and

Heremod are introduced to give us a standard of comparison for Beowulf.

Lines 916-1008a. Men come from far and near to see Grendel's arm. Hrothgar appears and, as might be expected, makes a speech and promises a splendid reward. Beowulf replies and apologizes for letting Grendel get away. Unferth looks upon the arm and has nothing to say. Then Heorot is prepared for a feast to celebrate the victory. The damage to the hall is stressed (only the roof is undamaged), and Grendel's fate is discussed for the third or fourth time: ". . . the fierce fighter *(aglæca)* . . . turned in flight, despairing of life. That [the inevitable hour] is not easy to flee, but each bearer of a soul, driven by necessity, must seek the spot prepared where his body, fast on its final bed, sleeps after the banquet" (lines 1003-1008). It may be mere sentimentality to read into these lines some pity even for the fate of Grendel, but certainly they express a melancholy awareness of the lot of all mortals. Grendel had been a fierce fighter (the kind most admired in a society of warriors), and he had come to the end of the road that all warriors must travel. After the first fury of battle has worn off, the vengeful references to his fate in hell are replaced by reflective melancholy. Like many of the other recurrences to the same subject in *Beowulf,* this is not mere repetition.

In passing, we must protest the glossing of the word *aglæca* by some editors as "champion" or "hero," when it applies to Beowulf and as "fiend" or "monster" when it applies to Grendel. That is simply cheating. Words, it is true, change meaning as the context changes, but not in this way. In either of these contexts, *aglæca* must mean "champion," "fierce fighter," or "terrible opponent." As applied to Grendel, it shows an appreciation of his fighting qualities. One does not enhance a hero's glory by belittling his adversaries.

Lines 1008b-62. At the feast, Hrothgar bestows on Beowulf weapons and eight horses with magnificent trappings, bestows appropriate gifts on Beowulf's surviving companions, and pays wergild (compensation) for the one eaten by Grendel. The passage concludes with gnomic-elegiac observations on the power of God and the experiences a man must endure before he arrives at wisdom.

Lines 1063-1159a. The feast begins, and Hrothgar's scop sings the lay of Finn. Like Beowulf's prediction of the outcome of the marriage of Freawaru and Ingeld (lines 2032-66), the lay is an account of the revival of a feud after a peace sealed by a royal marriage. This tale has no obvious relation to the main story and may be there merely to indicate the elegance of the entertainment.

Lines 1159b-87. After the song Wealhtheow appears and approaches Hrothgar and Hrothulf, who, we are told rather ominously, are *still* at peace with each other. Unferth sits at Hrothgar's feet; both Hrothgar and Hrothulf trust him. Wealhtheow offers wine to Hrothgar and exhorts him to be generous to the Geats. Then—rather tactlessly, it seems— she exhorts Hrothgar to enjoy life while he can and (as a result of his generosity?) to leave a kingdom to his heirs. Hrothulf, she says, will remember all the benefits that she and Hrothgar have bestowed upon him and be kind to their children.

Lines 1188-1231. Wealhtheow then turns to Beowulf, offers him the cup, and bestows on him a ring so splendid that it is compared with the necklace of the —unidentified— Brosings (with a brief, not very clear reference to Hama and Eormanric), and a tracing of its later history. She then asks Beowulf to befriend her sons and concludes this remarkable speech with a panegyric on the perfect harmony and loyalty that reign in the Danish court. The lady protests a great deal too much.

None of this passage contributes much to the main story, but it is important to what might be called the subplot of the first part of the poem: the fortunes of the Danish royal house. Concord among Danes is not destined to endure. From a brief allusion in *Widsith* we may assume that Hrothulf remained true to Hrothgar until after they had defeated Ingeld. Thereafter, according to Scandinavian tradition, Hrothulf seized the throne from Hrothgar and was later slain by Hrothgar's son, who in turn was slain by one of his cousins.

Wealhtheow's tactlessness may be merely the poet's device for alluding to these events, or it may be effective character depiction. Wealhtheow may be a mother so obsessed by the desire to secure the succession of her son that she does not realize the harm she is doing. Under Germanic law, the council of elders (Witan) or the warriors of the tribe were supposed to elect as king the ablest member of the royal house, and Wealhtheow's attempt to forestall the election of Hrothulf may have led to exactly the troubles she wished to avoid. Unferth's part in these events is unknown to us, but it is obviously known to the poet and his audience and is obviously discreditable.

Lines 1232–55a. The feast continues in joyous forgetfulness of previous sorrows (and without premonition of new sorrow near at hand). Hrothgar and Beowulf depart and leave the Danes to hold the hall. The author comments on how they sleep with their arms ready to hand and praises their discipline and organization—another example of his desire to maintain the reputation of Hrothgar and the Danes in spite of their inability to defend Heorot (but one, he remarks parenthetically, is to pay dear for his night's sleep).

Lines 1255b–1306a. Grendel's mother still lives to pursue the blood feud (Grendel's descent from Cain and his defeat at Heorot are brought up again). She comes to Heorot, and the Danes spring to arms. She flees "to save her life," but not before she has seized Æschere, Hrothgar's dearest companion, and carried him off, snatching down Grendel's arm and taking it with her as she departs. Lest we should blame Beowulf, we are told that he was sleeping elsewhere. The author concludes with the curiously neutral remark that it was a bad quarrel for which both sides must pay with the lives of friends. Either he regards both sides as about equally justified, or he is expressing himself formulaically. In fact, the whole brief passage seems a little flat and perfunctory. Probably the author realized that a second fight in the hall might be an anticlimax and wisely got through it as fast as possible.

Lines 1306b–44. Hrothgar appears and has Beowulf summoned. At this point Beowulf's one rather unavoidable lapse from perfect courtliness occurs. Being ignorant of what has happened, he asks whether Hrothgar has slept well. Hrothgar replies that this is no time to talk of pleasant things: an avenger has come because of Beowulf's slaying of Grendel. Then, turning on his hall thanes, he reminds them that they will no longer receive the gifts that Æschere was wont to bestow on them. One gets the impression that he blames both Beowulf and the thanes—not a very rational attitude, but grief is not rational, and there is no one else at hand to blame.

Lines 1345–82. Hrothgar goes on to say that his people had reported seeing two creatures, "mighty moor steppers," one male and one female. His description of their haunt—an estuary or sea-loch—is one of the high points of the poem. So terrible is the mere that the stag pursued by hounds will turn and die on the bank rather than save his life by taking to the water. Hrothgar's concluding "nis þæt heoru stow!" (that is not a good place, line 1372b) is not only a very early example—one of many in *Beowulf*—of the English habit of litotes but also the most striking. Then Hrothgar appeals to Beowulf as the only one who can bring the feud to a successful conclusion and promises proper reward if he does so.

Lines 1383-89. Beowulf's reply is characteristic of the warrior code: "Sorrow not, wise man, it is better for any man to avenge his friend than to mourn too much. Each of us must reach the end of life. Let him who may achieve glory after death. That is best for the dead."

Lines 1390-1441a. Danes and Geats set out for the mere through very wild country. As a final grim touch, they discover Æschere's head on the bank of the mere, which is still blood-stained. The monsters of the mere are disturbed and swim off—all but one, which is shot with an arrow and finished off with a boar spear.

Lines 1441b-72. Beowulf makes ready. For this undertaking he wears his byrnie and helm, which are described in some detail, and bears the sword Hrunting, lent him by Unferth. Hrunting, as the author's description shows, is a splendid weapon—a pattern-welded sword, hardened in the blood of battle. Never has it failed its bearer in war. Beowulf accepts the loan with gratitude, but the author cannot resist a jab at Unferth: "Indeed the son of Ecglaf, mighty in strength, had forgotten what he had spoken, flushed with liquor, when he lent the weapon to a better swordsman. He himself dared not venture his life under the sea surges to perform mighty deeds. There he lost glory, a reputation for valor."

This comment is thoroughly unfair. Since Unferth did not have the might of thirty men in his handgrip and could not, so far as we know, stay alive indefinitely under water, what he was refusing was not a chance for glory but an opportunity to be eaten by Grendel's mother—an experience that none of the Danes or even of Beowulf's Geats was eager to undergo. Either the author feels a special animus toward Unferth, or he is emphasizing his hero's greatness by contrasting him with a champion noted for cleverness and strength.

Lines 1473–91. Beowulf makes his will. If battle takes him, Hrothgar is to protect his thanes. The treasures already given him are to go to Hygelac. And a splendid sword (Beowulf's own?) is to go to Unferth, that famous man (*widcud'ne man,* line 1489). "As for myself, I will achieve fame with Hrunting, or death shall take me" (lines 1490-91).

Lines 1492–1528. The preliminaries to the second fight have been much briefer than those for the first (a little less than two hundred lines), and without more ado Beowulf plunges into the mere. He sinks for a long time. At the bottom he is seized by Grendel's dam, who has perceived his coming, and is dragged into her hall, which the water does not enter. Ironically enough, his struggle with what the poet calls the weaker female of the species is far more perilous than that with Grendel. Only his good byrnie saves him, first from her claws, which she tries to drive through his body; next from the tusks of the sea beasts that gather to attack him and break some links of the byrnie; and finally

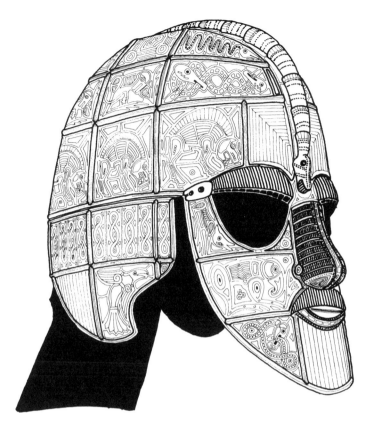

The Sutton Hoo helmet is too corroded for the designs of the individual plates to be readily identifiable, and so the artist has supplied designs from contemporary Anglo-Saxon work and suggestions from Beowulf *("besette swinlicum"—decorated with pictures of boars—line 1453). The shape of the structure shown in the drawing above is that of the Sutton Hoo helmet. The ridge at the top of the helmet is the "wala" (line 1031). Courtesy of the Trustees of the British Museum.*

from her *seax* (dagger). In her hall he has the opportunity to strike her with Hrunting, which will not "bite" on his adversary (the first time, the author informs us parenthetically, that it has failed in battle).

Lines 1529–1605a. Beowulf casts aside Hrunting and grapples with Grendel's mother, who pins him down and strikes him with her *seax,* but his byrnie holds. Beowulf breaks free and seizes from the wall a mighty sword, the work of giants, too large for any other man to wield, and in desperation strikes with it. The blow shears through the neck of Grendel's mother, but Beowulf does not relax his vigilance. He cannot be sure that Grendel is dead, and he does not know what other monsters may lurk in the hall. He clutches the sword and proceeds to investigate. Come what may, he is going to settle the account with Grendel for good and all. Here the author pauses to recapitulate Grendel's crimes. Then Beowulf finds Grendel lying dead by the wall and in a burst of fury strikes off his head.

In this fury some commentators think that they see an example of berserk rage. The theory is unconvincing, particularly since there is a much more plausible explanation. The berserk works himself into a crazy rage *before* the battle. Beowulf becomes furious after the battle is won. Rage is a natural reaction to a bad fright. Beowulf had struck his last blow against Grendel's mother in almost hopeless desperation (*aldres orwena,* despairing of life, line 1565).[1] The blow that decapitates Grendel is a release of this pent-up terror. Nowhere else do we see more clearly that Beowulf is a mortal man—not a fearless demigod—than in this passage. For such a man courage is more often the conquest of fear than the absence of it.

Lines 1605b–22. The blade of the sword melts away like an icicle in the sun, dissolved by Grendel's blood. Taking only the hilt of the sword and Grendel's head as trophies, Beowulf swims back to the surface. The mere is cleansed.

Lines 1623–98a. By the time he reaches the surface, the Danes have given up hope and gone home. Beowulf's retainers, who have hoped but not expected to see their lord again, have waited faithfully. They greet him joyfully and relieve him of his arms. Then they set out for Heorot with four men laboring to carry the head of Grendel attached to a spear shaft. When they reach Heorot, the head is borne into the hall, "terrible before the earls," and Beowulf tells his story. Hrothgar examines the hilt and its strange runes that tell a tale of ancient strife and the name of the first owner.

Lines 1698b–1768. Hrothgar praises Beowulf, contrasts him to Heremod (perhaps as a warning), and indulges in another gnomic-elegiac speech on the brevity of human joy and the danger that the fortunate man may fall victim to arrogance *(oferhygd).* Such a man becomes avaricious and dies despised and deserted, leaving his hoarded wealth for another to enjoy (a commonplace in Christian homilies). He then warns Beowulf not to be puffed up by temporary good fortune. All too soon fire, flood, or the sword will carry him off, or old age will slay him.

Lines 1769–98. Hrothgar then cites his own example. For fifty years he had ruled the Danes, conquering neighboring peoples until he held no adversary under heaven of any account. Then Grendel came to humble his pride until Beowulf came to his rescue. Thus Hrothgar finds a gracious ending for what would otherwise have been a rather ungracious lecture. Then, in quick summary, we are told that there are feast and song, after which all retire to bed.

Lines 1799-1887. In the morning Beowulf returns Hrunting to Unferth with proper thanks. He announces that it is time for the Geats to depart, praises the entertainment they have received at Heorot and the generous gifts of Hrothgar, promises to come to his aid again if need should arise, and ends by inviting Hrothgar's son Hrethric to visit the Geatish court. Hrothgar replies, praising Beowulf, predicting a great future for him, and promising that the old hostility of Geats and Danes shall be ended. He bestows twelve (unspecified) gifts on Beowulf, and they bid each other a farewell saddened by Hrothgar's belief that he will never see Beowulf again.

The second battle and its aftermath are handled with both economy and variety. Repetitious events are cut short. The combat is of an entirely different kind. The inevitable speeches in the hall deal with different subjects. Wealhtheow's speech is used to reveal the seeds of dissension and treachery in the Danish court, and Hrothgar's for moralizing and reminiscence (on the treatment of the second gift giving, see chapter 9 below).

Lines 1888-1926. Beowulf's return to the ship and his voyage home require only forty lines. For some reason we are given a description of Hygelac's court before we come to Beowulf's arrival. Almost the whole of this passage is taken up with a comparison between Hygd, Hygelac's queen, and Thryth (or Modthryth), queen of Offa the Elder, King of the Angles before their migration to England.

The Thryth passage is the most troublesome in the whole poem—so troublesome, in fact, that some scholars suggest that it has been mutilated by the loss of a number of lines and others have considered it an interpolation. The fact that the description of the court precedes Beowulf's appearance there may support the idea that something has happened to the text, such as the copying of a loose leaf of an exemplar in the wrong place by a careless scribe or an inept interpolation.

Lines 1927-62. Hygd, we are told, is young but behaves just as a queen should, unlike Thryth, who, before she was married, would encompass the torture and death of any man who so much as looked at her. After her father married her to Offa, however, she became a reformed character.

At first glance Thryth may seem, like Heremod, to be merely a bad character introduced to heighten the virtues of a good one by contrast, but the more one considers the passage, the less satisfactory such an explanation becomes. As a queen Thryth seems to have been satisfactory, if not admirable. Why contrast her conduct as a princess with that of Hygd as a queen? For that matter, why introduce her at all? She serves no such purpose as Wealhtheow in developing a point in which the poet is obviously interested, and although Hygd is briefly mentioned in the second part of the poem, there seems to be no special reason for developing her character here.

The theory that the allusion to Thryth and Offa was included, originally or as an interpolation, as a compliment to Offa of Mercia is not particularly satisfactory either. Fame as a Petruchio is not the sort of glory that a monarch of the Heptarchy would much desire, particularly since a truly heroic theme—the elder Offa's single-handed victory over the Swabians—should have been available to the poet. To read the piece as a sort of political allegory referring to Offa of Mercia and his queen Cynethrith is equally unsatisfactory. Poets among the Germanic tribes did not enjoy the immunity apparently conferred on Celtic bards, and they would have found propaganda of this sort a dangerous and unprofitable business. This appears to be one of those times when an admission of ignorance of the point of a passage is the wisest course.

Lines 1963–98. Once Beowulf reaches the court, things clear up. Hygelac is glad to see him back. He had feared that Grendel would be too much for Beowulf and had advised Beowulf to let the Danes settle their own problems. This picture of the rather gruff affection of the two kinsmen is one of the most human passages in the poem.

Lines 1999–2069. Beowulf's reply is neither a summary nor a repetition of what has gone before. After remarking that he has taken care of Grendel, he goes on to describe the splendors of the Danish court and introduces an entirely new subject: the presence of Ingeld, prince of the Heatho-Bards, who has been betrothed to Hrothgar's daughter Freawaru in an attempt to heal a feud between the Danes and the Heatho-Bards. He goes on to observe that in his opinion that sort of thing is unlikely to work and gives a very concrete illustration of how such a peace is likely to break down. This passage has been the subject of much discussion, but its general intent is clear enough. Beowulf is reporting to his king on a matter of political concern. Peace or war between Danes and Bards will be of import to the Geats.

Lines 2069–2100. Next Beowulf reports in more detail on his fight with Grendel. The passage is an excellent example of the author's method of incremental repetition. In it we learn for the first time the name of the Geat devoured by Grendel—Hondscio (Glove). Before, his name was of no great interest, but Beowulf can hardly report his death to Hygelac without naming him. The name is atypical and has aroused some speculation. It is unlikely that the name of such a rather unimportant character would be preserved by tradition, and the author may have invented it for the occasion, but why he should have chosen this particular name is not clear.

Much more striking is the grisly game bag that hung at Grendel's belt or from his shoulder to hold such of his prey as he did not eat on the spot. It was a notable piece of leatherwork, made of dragon skin and curiously adorned. Beowulf observes with grim irony that Grendel planned to put him in it but that things did not work out that way. Perhaps this bit of description was omitted from the account of the fight to keep from slowing up the action. The rest of the fight is described in a few lines.

Lines 2101-66a. Next Beowulf tells briefly of the rewards given him and the feasting in the hall (with special reference to Hrothgar's reminiscences), the attack by Grendel's mother, his fight with her, and the further rewards given him by Hrothgar. He wishes, he continues, to give this booty to Hygelac: "All my favors have come from thee; I have few near kinsmen save, Hygelac, thee" (lines 2149-50). The gifts are then brought in, including a particularly magnificent sword, an heirloom of the Danish king Hiorogar, which Hrothgar had sent as a special gift to Hygelac.

Lines 2166-71. The gift giving is interrupted by a gnomic passage: "So should a man do. By no means with secret craft weave a net of plots for another, prepare the death of a comrade. To the valiant Hygelac his nephew was very loyal, and each was mindful of the favors of the other."

Lines 2172-76. Hygd, the wife of Hygelac, is given her share of the treasure: the necklace given to Beowulf by Wealhtheow and three splendid horses (we are not told how or why the necklace came to be worn by Hygelac on his fatal Frisian raid).

Lines 2177–89. The poet reverts to a favorite theme: Beowulf won fame through mighty deeds, but he did not slay his hearth companions in drunken rage; although he was the strongest of mankind, he was benevolent. Then, suddenly and rather needlessly, he tells of Beowulf's unpromising youth. This trick of including something nonessential that strikes his fancy may explain the poet's inclusion of the Thryth episode. Doubtless such allusive digressions were regarded as adornments rather than defects by contemporary audiences.

Lines 2190–99. Finally Hygelac has brought in a national treasure (the heirloom of Hrethel; no better sword was owned by the Geats) and lays it across Beowulf's knees. This may be the sword Nægling, which appears in the second part of the poem. Hygelac bestows on Beowulf seven thousand hides of land (about the proper hidage for a subkingdom under the Heptarchy) and gives him a hall and a throne (a hide was enough land to support a peasant family). In other words, he makes him a subregulus. Thereafter they rule their land together with Hygelac as chief king.

Here the poet might have concluded, "And they all lived happily ever afterwards." But reigns during the Heptarchy were seldom long and never peaceful.

Taken as a whole, the first part of Beowulf has a sound structure: an introduction that sets the stage for the hero, his two exploits in Denmark, and a brief epilogue, his triumphant return home. Through this main story run certain subthemes. One is the glory of the Scyldings and their misfortunes. The first of these disasters, the burning of Heorot, greatest of halls, is hinted at very early in the poem and is recalled to the minds of the audience by the extended reference to Ingeld, the burner of Heorot, near the end. An even grimmer subject, the mutual destruction of the Scyldings through treachery to each other, is foreshadowed by the passage on Hrothgar, Hrothulf, Unferth, and Wealhtheow after the slaying of Grendel's mother.

On this last point the Geats present a striking contrast to the Danes, particularly if we consider certain events in the second part of the poem. Unlike Wealhtheow, who is so obsessed by securing the succession of her sons to the throne that she creates an atmosphere of suspicion and hostility, Hygd asks Beowulf to take the throne for the good of the kingdom after the death of Hygelac. Unlike Hrothulf, who seizes his uncle's throne, Beowulf will not take the throne, as he would have every right to do, but instead becomes regent for Heardred and accepts the throne only after Heardred is dead and the line of Hygelac has run out. For one so fond of moralizing, the author does little to stress this contrast. Nevertheless, it is there. The theme of loyalty and the wickedness of plots that appears not only in this passage but also in Beowulf's summing up of his life (lines 2738-43) may be an oblique comment on Danish perfidy.

A point that the author does stress is the obligation to benevolence and the wickedness of allowing one's strength and fame to make him cruel and avaricious. This moral is enforced by the two references to Heremod; possibly by the allusion to Thryth, in her youth a sort of female counterpart to Heremod; and by the author's summing up of Beowulf's virtues in lines 2177-83. It is also the note on which Beowulf closes.

CHAPTER 6

The Story: Beowulf as King

THE central event of the second part of *Beowulf* is Beowulf's fight with a dragon that is ravaging his kingdom. In this fight the dragon is killed and Beowulf mortally wounded. Concomitant events are the plundering of the dragon's hoard (a requisite in a Germanic dragon story) and Beowulf's funeral.

This part differs from the first in both subject matter and technique. The Danes disappear from the story. Digressions are drawn from the history of the Geats, not from tales of earlier heroes, and are used to fill in the gap of about fifty years between Beowulf's return from Heorot and his encounter with the dragon. Yet there are also common elements in the two parts. In the second part the author again foreshadows events later in the story and events that occur after the end of the story proper. For example, before the dragon fight he tells us that this fight will be the end of both Beowulf and the dragon, and the messenger who announces Beowulf's death to the people makes it clear that this will mean the end of the Geats. Beowulf is still the resolute slayer of monsters, but he is more the mortal man and less the adventurous young demigod. In the first part he seeks out strife; in the last it is thrust upon him.

Beowulf's death has been the cause of a good deal of unenlightened comment. Some scholars consider it the result of hubris, and others have attributed it to his greed for gold. Certain commentators believe that if Beowulf had not been killed by the dragon the kingdom of the Geats would never have fallen. If the author had continued the story beyond the return from Denmark, he might, of course, have had Beowulf kill the dragon while he was still a comparatively young man and left him to live happily ever afterward. But unless the author had managed to make a good deal more of the dragon fight than he does in this story, it would have added little to the length of the work and would have been something of an anticlimax after Beowulf's feats at Heorot. The author might also have given us a chronicle of Beowulf's feats after his return from Heorot and concluded with a victorious dragon fight, but it is hard to see how he could have made much of such a story artistically. Or he could have ended his tale with Beowulf's forsaking the world to become a monk or hermit, as did more than one English king. But we—and his audience—might have felt that such a conclusion did not quite fit the tone of the rest of the story or the character of Beowulf. A pious death in bed was not a suitable ending for such a hero.

Yet in a way the last section of *Beowulf* does parallel the conclusion of a saint's life, in which a "good death" is almost obligatory. Examples of such deaths can be seen in Bede's account of the death of Caedmon and in Cuthbert's account of the death of Bede. For a hero-king the best death imaginable is death in a battle fought to save his people, and that is the death the poet gives Beowulf.

To state that his was a death incurred through hubris or a lust for gold that laid his people open to the attacks of the Franks and the Swedes is to place a very peculiar interpretation on the facts. Beowulf must have been twenty or thereabouts when he visited Heorot. After that visit he lived through the reigns of Hygelac and Heardred and then ruled for fifty years. Even if we consider "fifty years" a round number instead of an exact period, Beowulf was an old man at the time of the dragon fight. Unless the author proposed to make him live as long as an antediluvian patriarch, he could not have lived much longer. Sooner or later the Geats would have to face their enemies unprotected by the might of Beowulf's arm and the terror of his name whether or not he survived the dragon fight. And if the dragon had not been killed, there would have been no Geats left to face the Swedes. Beowulf's duty was to deal with the immediate danger, and, as usual, he did his duty.[1]

If there is hubris involved in the fate of the Geats, it was that of Hygelac, who out of pride asked for trouble with the Frisians ("for wlenco wean ahsode," line 1206) and led most of his host to death, or that of Hygelac and Heardred, who embroiled their people in Swedish wars of succession that led to the defeat and death of Heardred. Beowulf had taken over a weakened and defeated people and given them many years of comparative peace and security. If, once saved from the dragon, they were not able to stand on their own feet, they never would be.

Summary

Lines 2200-2323. The second part summarizes in ten lines the death of Hygelac, the fall of his son Heardred, and Beowulf's reign of fifty years (lines 2200-10). Then we come to the depredations of the dragon. They were caused by the theft of a cup from the dragon's hoard by a servant who fled the wrath of his lord, stumbled upon the dragon's lair in an ancient barrow, and took the cup to appease his master. We are told how the last of a mighty race had buried this treasure in the barrow. The dragon had discovered the hoard and settled down contentedly to guard it. For three hundred years he had remained undisturbed. Then the cup was stolen, and the dragon began ravaging Beowulf's realm with fire. Like Grendel he went abroad by night and stayed in his lair by day.

Lines 2324-54. Beowulf learns of the dragon's raids, one of which has destroyed his own royal hall, and fears that he has unknowingly angered the Lord. Beowulf orders an iron shield made for him. He disdains to bring an army against the dragon because he has survived many desperate adventures since he cleansed Heorot. This observation may be interpreted to imply hubris, but it might more reasonably be said to indicate that Beowulf planned to use a method which had served him well in the past.

Lines 2354-96. From the reference to Beowulf's former valor the author leads by a smooth transition to Beowulf's part in Hygelac's Frisian raid and another marvelous aquatic feat—swimming home with thirty panoplies of armor on his arm (lines 2360-62). *Hildegeatwa* may mean only byrnies, but it could just as well mean helmets and byrnies and, perhaps, shields. Here the author maintains the same ratio between Beowulf's powers and those of an ordinary man, as when he says earlier that Beowulf has the might of thirty men in his handgrip (lines 379-81), though it may be doubtful how many ordinary men could swim in full armor.

After this comes Hygd's request that Beowulf accept the throne, and his refusal to supplant Hygelac's son Heardred. Heardred's involvement in Swedish dynastic struggles, his consequent death, and Beowulf's part in the deposing of Onela, king of the Swedes, are dealt with in a few lines. Plainly these are matters on which the poet does not wish to elaborate but on which he feels that he should fill in the record.

Lines 2397–2489. The poet returns to the main story. Beowulf and eleven companions seek out the dragon's den, guided by the serf who stole the cup. Beowulf sits down and makes a long speech in which he looks back over his life from the time when, at the age of seven, he became the fosterling of Hrethel, king of the Geats. He tells of the sorrow of Hrethel when his oldest son, Herebeald, was accidentally killed by another son, Hæthcyn, and of the sorrow of a father who cannot avenge his son, illustrated by the tale of an old man whose son has been hanged. Then he tells of Hrethel's death from sorrow and of an earlier stage in the Swedish-Geatish troubles in which Hæthcyn was slain and Hygelac avenged him with the death of Onela.

Whitelock suggests that this passage, which the modern reader finds difficult to follow because it alludes briefly to events otherwise unrecorded, may have been introduced to pad out the second part of the story. The dragon fight by itself would be a slight counterpoise to the two combats at Heorot. Whatever its purpose, the passage is brought in naturally enough. Beowulf senses that this will be his last fight. Although he does not flinch from it, he is in no hurry to rush upon his fate. Instead, he pauses to gather strength and resolution by looking back over a life of valiant deeds.

Lines 2490–2509. The next part of the speech, in which Beowulf recounts how he repaid Hygelac's favors and alludes to his killing of the Frankish Dæghræfn, is in the same vein.

Lines 2510–37. Beowulf delivers his concluding *beotword:* "Many a battle I survived in youth; yet will I, ancient guardian of the people, pursue the feud, perform mighty deeds if the wicked slayer will venture from his den" (lines 2510-15). The lines have been compared with those of Tennyson's Ulysses: "Death closes all. But something ere the end, / some deed of noble note may yet be done." Beowulf's description of himself as "guardian of the people" (*folces weard,* line 2513) is significant. He is not on a mere treasure hunt; he is defending his subjects. He regrets that he cannot fight the dragon bare-handed and orders his retainers to withdraw because he plans to fight the dragon alone. As before his previous fights, he proclaims his intention to conquer or die.

Lines 2538-65. Beowulf advances toward the entrance to the dragon's barrow and with a mighty shout challenges it to battle. The dragon comes forth and looks upon Beowulf. Each recognizes the other as a perilous opponent: "Each of the enemies feared the other" (line 2565). Dragons, except for their peculiar fixation in the matter of treasure, are sagacious beasts (one, Fafnir, carries on a conversation with Sigurd in the *Fáfnismál*—part of the Old Norse *Elder Edda*),[2] and the dragon realizes that Beowulf is no ordinary opponent.

Lines 2566-91. The dragon advances, and Beowulf finds his iron shield less protection than he had hoped against the dragon's fiery breath. Nevertheless, he strikes the dragon with his sword, but Nægling will not bite on the dragon's bony crest. Infuriated by the blow, the dragon belches even fiercer fire, and Beowulf is forced to step back (a contradiction of his *beotword:* "I will not flee the guardian of the hoard by a foot's breadth," line 2525—a formula that appears elsewhere in Old English poetry).

Lines 2592-2630. Once more the opponents come together. All but one of Beowulf's companions flee to the woods. The young hero who remains is Wiglaf, Beowulf's nephew. Here the poet pauses to give us something of Wiglaf's pedigree and a history of his sword, the Heirloom of Eanmund (to the audience of *Beowulf* one was probably as important as the other; a great sword might outlast many bearers). To some modern readers this may not seem exactly the place to pause to consider pedigrees, but a contemporary of the poet would see nothing incongruous in the passage. If we wish to justify it in modern critical terms, we may say that a pause in the action just here heightens the suspense.

Lines 2631–68. Next comes a rather long speech in which Wiglaf states his intention of repaying Beowulf's former favors by going to his aid. On the convention of such speeches, see chapter 7.

Lines 2669–2710. With his incurable addiction to direct action, Beowulf once more lets fall his blade on the dragon's invulnerable crest, and Nægling is shattered to bits. The dragon rears up and seizes Beowulf by the neck, and Wiglaf, using point instead of edge, thrusts his sword into the softer underparts that the dragon has exposed, so that its fiery breath slackens: "He struck somewhat lower down, so that his sword plunged [*gedeaf*]" (lines 2699–2700). The verb *gedeaf* pictures the sword sliding into the dragon as a diver slides through the surface of the water. With a last mighty effort Beowulf draws his *seax* and cuts the dragon in two.

The dragon is dead, and Beowulf mortally wounded. One might think that the poem was nearing its end, but almost half of the last section of the poem (470 lines) is still to come. How well the author sustains the interest of this passage is a matter of opinion, but to most students of the poem he seems to do so rather well. So far as a contemporary audience is concerned, we can only guess, but apparently

the author assumes that they want the story fully rounded
out.

Lines 2711–51. After Wiglaf has bathed Beowulf's wound,
the old hero is able to speak. He laments that he has no son
to whom to leave his armor, but he is glad that he held the
throne for fifty winters and protected his people. He rejoices
that he has not indulged in plots or sworn false oaths and
that the Lord will have no occasion to accuse him of the
slaughter of kinsmen (a recurrent deed of others in the
poem).[3] Then he orders Wiglaf to search the barrow and
bring out the dragon's hoard so that he can see it.

Lines 2752–2820. Wiglaf enters the barrow, whose contents are described at some length, and hurries back to Beowulf with a load of treasure. Beowulf rejoices that he has
been able to win such a treasure for his people and gives
instructions for his funeral pyre and barrow. Then he bestows his jewels and armor on Wiglaf, the last of his kin,
and his soul departs "to seek the judgment of the righteous"
(line 2820).

Lines 2821–45. The author describes Beowulf and the dragon lying dead side by side and observes rather sententiously
that it was a bad business fighting with a dragon or disturbing
his hoard. Beowulf, he adds, had paid for the treasure with
his life. Some commentators seem to consider this passage,
combined with Wiglaf's remarks about Beowulf's insistence
on fighting the dragon alone as a criticism of Beowulf's conduct. Beowulf's tactics may be open to criticism, but it is
hard to see how he could have saved his people without
fighting the dragon, and this was not an age in which a
commander "led his regiment from behind." It is true that
the poet shifts the emphasis of his tale from Beowulf's de-

A drawing of the great Sutton Hoo brooch, revealing the stunning interlace complexity of the design characteristic of Celtic and Anglo-Saxon art. Some such designs must be imagined when the Beowulf *poet speaks of the golden treasures Hrothgar gave to Beowulf and those discovered in the dragon's barrow. Courtesy of the Trustees of the British Museum.*

fense of his realm to his winning of the dragon's hoard, but he can hardly have forgotten Beowulf's original purpose. Possibly he felt that Beowulf realized that his people would need treasure after he was gone. Some commentators profess to see Beowulf's fate as a result of a curse on the dragon's gold. Perhaps they are influenced by similar curses in later legends. Taken by themselves, the author's statements are rather ambiguous. Sigemund seems to have come to no harm as a result of plundering a dragon's hoard (lines 884-97). In fact, if we can take the "he pæs ær ond'ah" of line 900 as referring to this episode, he profited by it. Lines 2836-45 state that no man, no matter how valiant, who challenged the dragon was likely to profit by the encounter and that Beowulf had bought the dragon's hoard with his life. Whether this implies a curse that results in the later fate of the Geats is debatable. A dragon was a sufficiently formidable adversary to guarantee trouble for whoever challenged him without the assistance of a curse.

It is only in lines 3051-57 that a protective spell is mentioned: "the gold of the men of old, wrapped in a spell so that no man could disturb that ring hall unless God himself . . . had granted to whom he would . . . to open the hoard, even to such a man as seemed fitting to him."

Lines 3058-75. With his customary impartiality the author then goes on to blame the dragon: "Then it was plain that it did not profit him who unrighteously hid treasure within a wall. The guardian had slain one of a few; then the feud was swiftly avenged." Next the author embroiders an idea also found in an Arab saying: "No man knoweth where his grave is dug" (lines 3062b-65). Beowulf did not know when he challenged the dragon how his end would come. Considering that he depicts Beowulf as fey throughout the first part of this episode, the author seems to be contradicting himself, as in one or two other passages in which he indulges in incremental repetition. Having begun with a straightforward dragon fight in the Sigemund manner, he bethinks him that there may have been a spell or curse involved. He does, however, put in an escape clause: "Thus the mightly lords who put that [the treasure] there solemnly declared that that man who disturbed that place should be guilty of sin, harried by a pagan curse, fast in the bonds of hell, tormented by evil *unless the one desirous of gold was assured of the Lord's favor*"(italics ours, lines 3069-75).

Twice in this passage (lines 3054-57, 3074-75) the author implies that the Lord can cancel the curse, just as he states (lines 696-702 and elsewhere) that the Lord granted Beowulf victory over Grendel. Since there is nothing anywhere else in the poem to imply that Beowulf is destined for the bonds of hell, we must assume that the curse has been at least partly negated. That it was completely so and that Beowulf's fate is simply a consequence of the dragon's *ellen* is a possible, if somewhat strained, interpretation. Another—also not entirely satisfactory—is that the curse, though negated in the hereafter, has retained some residual force in the here. The most plausible is that, like Homer, the author occasionally nods and that this is one of those occasions. A further inconsistency is that in the first account of the burying of the treasure there are no "mighty lords" but only one wretched survivor and that his speech contains no spell or curse.

Lines 2845-3027. When the cowardly retainers return, they are bitterly rebuked by Wiglaf, who then sends a messenger to inform the people of Beowulf's death. It is extremely unlikely that Wiglaf, who seems to have been a young man of some promise, would actually have sent such a bird of ill omen at a time when the Geats needed to gather all their strength and resolution to meet attacks that were sure to come. Plainly the author is using the messenger as a means to foreshadow the fate that he knew would soon overtake the Geats.

The messenger announces Beowulf's death and goes on to prophesy war with the Franks and the Swedes. In a long, rather difficult passage he relates the death of Ongentheow at the hands of the Geats. Not content with this, he says that all the treasure of the dragon's hoard will be laid on the pyre because the days of the Geats' power are over and nothing awaits them but poverty, captivity, exile, and death. Any commander who knew his business would, of course, have silenced this "wise man," as the poet calls him, with a noose around the neck.

Perhaps the poet wishes to show a decline in Geatish morale in the last section of the poem. Except for Wiglaf, Beowulf's retainers in the dragon fight are a sorry contrast to the thanes who stoically prepared to die with him in Heorot. An overconscientious commentator might speculate that the Geats had fallen into the habit of relying too much on Beowulf and too little on their own *ellen*—an early example of the demoralizing effects of paternalism. The decision to bury all the dearly won treasure in Beowulf's barrow may have been a magnificent gesture of grief, but it seems to run counter to Beowulf's expressed intention, and it certainly ignores the fact that the treasure could have paid for the hire of many a stout fighter to strengthen the Geats in the perilous days ahead.

Lines 3028-3100. After the messenger's speech the people go to look upon Beowulf and the dragon and the treasure from the hoard. Then follows the digression on the spell or curse protecting the hoard (lines 3052-75). Not content with the implication that Beowulf has been guilty of sin or rashness in ordering the plundering of the hoard (lines 3076-81), the author goes on to suggest that Beowulf has been guilty of something like hubris. He does, however, put this accusation into the mouth of Wiglaf, who is in the grip of irrational emotion, instead of stating it in his own person. Many must suffer, says Wiglaf, because of the decision of one man. His companions had been unable to persuade Beowulf to let the dragon alone, to let him lie where he had long dwelt until the end of the world.

This is a thoroughly unreasonable speech. The dragon was not lying quietly in his cave; he was ravaging Beowulf's kingdom, and there is no hint elsewhere in the poem that he had any intent of ceasing to do so. If Beowulf was not to acquiesce supinely in the destruction of his people, his only choice was one of the means by which he should prevent it. Possibly the author expected his audience to recognize this speech as a mere outburst of feeling. If not, he was inviting more of the same sort of confusion as results from his belated consideration of the curse on the dragon's gold. Perhaps he yielded to the temptation to get every possible theme into the poem. Hubris *(ofermod)* is certainly an accepted theme in Old English poetry, but it is almost as hard to believe that the author would seriously accuse Beowulf of hubris as it is to think that he considered him destined for the bonds of hell. Lines 3050-86 seem to present Beowulf's character in a light so inconsistent with that of the rest of the poem that one leaves them with considerable relief.

Lines 3101-82. The conclusion, the description of Beowulf's magnificent funeral, is a fitting conclusion to the story of such a hero. The only point that has troubled the commentators is the identity of the old woman who sang sadly beside his pyre. Some have tried to identify her as Hygd, others as a wife of Beowulf mentioned nowhere else in the poem. Almost certainly she is neither. An eyewitness account of a ship cremation by Swedish Vikings in Russia mentions an old woman who was mistress of ceremonies.[4] She does not seem to have been a close relative of the deceased. The old woman in *Beowulf* was doubtless performing a similar function.

The people then build Beowulf's barrow, and twelve warriors ride about it singing his praises: "They said that of the kings of this world he was the mildest and most compassionate of men, kindest to his people and most eager for glory."

Here, not in the confused and confusing passages on curses and hubris, we have the final summing up of Beowulf's character. Commenting on this summary, George Lyman Kittredge observed in his Harvard lectures that it struck a note to match that of the tale of Scyld with which the story opens—a note of exalted resignation comparable to that on which Tennyson's *Morte d'Arthur* closes: "And on the mere the wailing died away." Both kings have done all they can for their people. The worries and lamentations of the living fade into silence in the presence of the mighty dead.

Taken as a whole, the second part of *Beowulf* suffers, like many other sequels, in comparison with the first. A good deal of it appears to be "filler" that could be dispensed with, and lines 3051-85 appear to diverge from the central theme. Nevertheless, it does contribute to the total plan—the presentation of the heroic ideal—for it completes the picture. The young, successful prince becomes the king confronted with an enemy whom he did not seek and over whom he can win only a partial victory. It crowns a heroic life with a heroic death.

The picture so presented accords with that of the Old English elegy. Happiness and prosperity—all human goods

Reconstruction of a fairly typical barrow of the first millennium A.D. The hillock covers a stone structure that may contain several small rooms. The entryway is made of stone slabs marked by designs. Such a barrow may or may not have been used for burial. Beowulf's barrow was clearly intended as a monument, for the hero's cremation was quite a separate affair.

except, perhaps, fame—are transitory. Victories may sometimes be gained, but wars are never really won, and fate stands ever ready to sweep away the lives and works of men. The Christian answer was, of course, to seek the permanent bliss of heaven. The heroic answer, as embodied in *Beowulf,* is a valiant stoicism: "Do your utmost. A good name is all you can win in this world." Very much the same philosophy is summed up in the epitaph (perhaps legendary) of a cowboy: "Here lies Bronco Bill. He always done his damnedest." Angels, it was once observed in a different context, can do no more.

In the light of this philosophy, the "tragedy of the Geats" implicit in Beowulf's death, of which some commentators make a great deal, becomes less significant. All that any man can leave his heirs is a good name and a glorious example. If they cannot be wise and valiant in their own right, he cannot save them. Those who appear to think that if Beowulf could somehow have survived his contest with the dragon both he and the Geats would have survived forever should reread both the poem and history.

CHAPTER 7

The Background of *Beowulf*

THE sources of *Beowulf,* if we may call them that, are to be found in the very large body of Continental tradition that the English brought with them or acquired through continued contact with their European cousins (evidence of this continued contact includes the Old English *Genesis B,* which is an English translation of a Continental poem, and the appearance of a text of another such poem, the *Heliand,* in an English library).[1] For its content, aside from a few minor Christian touches, *Beowulf* relies completely on this inherited body of folklore and legendary-historical materials. Except for the lay of creation—a passage reminiscent of Caedmon's hymn—sung by the scop in Heorot early in the poem and the linking of Grendel with the race of Cain, all the digressions and allusions in *Beowulf,* as well as the main story, are Continental. When and by whom this diverse material was assembled in a single tale cannot be demonstrated, but it seems most likely that it was put together by a single man—the author of *Beowulf.*

The materials from which *Beowulf* was assembled were from very different strata. The oldest stratum, which the poet probably did not recognize clearly for what it was, was pagan belief. The Danish genealogy (more likely, in fact, a list of what Bede called *bretwaldas*—that is, kings paramount—of Denmark and the Scandinavian peninsula) with which *Beowulf* opens is a compressed form of the genealogy more or less standard for English as well as Continental monarchs. The earlier members of these lists are pagan deities: Woden (Odin), Balder, Geat, and others. Curiously enough, Woden, the nexus in whom the various lines converge as we go back in time, does not begin most of these lists. He is preceded by Scyld, Beau(w), and others, and a count of generations places him quite late, probably in the fifth century. Whether the author of *Beowulf* omitted Woden merely to compress the list or to expunge the name of a heathen divinity is not certain.

In Scyld Scefing (Shield Son of the Sheaf), we may have traces of a culture hero who brought grain to man, and Beowulf himself may originally have been a Germanic Hercules, a slayer of monsters (particularly marine monsters) who, as he says of himself in one passage, made the sea safe for sailors. If the Beowulf in the Danish genealogy is anything more than a slip of the pen for Beaw (the common form in the king lists), he may have been such a hero, and the author or his sources may have transferred the qualities of one Beowulf to another.

Dragons, though they appear rather infrequently in literature, were a recognized part of early Germanic natural history (their habit of guarding hoards is noted in Old English gnomic verse). We might say that they were the equivalent of the modern coelacanth and okapi—rare beasts that were seldom seen but that everyone knew existed. As mentioned earlier, one of the digressions in *Beowulf* deals with the killing of a dragon by Sigemund.

Trolls, on the other hand, though well known in Scandinavia, do not seem to have become naturalized in English folklore, and it is doubtful whether the author of *Beowulf* recognized Grendel and his mother as of the troll kin. Yet they have two distinct troll characteristics: invulnerability to weapons and the inability to endure the light of day. If one wished to overcome a troll, he must either beat him with his bare hands by main strength or trick him into exposing himself to daylight, which would turn him to stone. Grendel's invulnerability is explained not as an innate characteristic but as the result of some special charm or spell (lines 800-805), and Beowulf's decision to fight him bare-handed is presented as a sporting gesture (lines 677-87), not as a necessary tactic. It appears that the author did not understand the original reason for this choice and put forward another explanation, which would further his purpose by emphasizing Beowulf's magnanimity.

Rather belatedly, during the dragon episode, the author brings in another explanation for Beowulf's unwillingness to use weapons: he had no luck with them because he was so strong that he always broke them (lines 2682-87). This looks like something out of a myth or a folktale—a special condition under which the hero must operate, like Antaeus's need to touch the earth or the vulnerability of Achilles' heel. Why the author does not bring up this point before the fight with Grendel is not clear. Still another folktale characteristic, brought in in isolation and, it seems, rather pointlessly, is Beowulf's sluggishness as a youth—a sort of ugly-duckling theme (lines 2183-84; see chapter 4).

For the inability of Grendel and his dam to harry the hall by daylight or to attack the Danes outside the hall the author wisely offers no explanation. One can offer only proximate, not ultimate, explanations for natural phenomena, and magic, if one accepts it, is a natural phenomenon. Inability to endure daylight is the mark of a troll. Limitation to a certain area is the mark of a tutelary spirit. Originally Grendel's attack on Heorot may have been considered a defense of his territorial rights, but in *Beowulf* it is said to result from his dislike of the sounds of rejoicing. If that were the only reason, it is hard to see why the Danes should have been safe if they stayed outside the hall. Once again, the author seems to be providing an explanation for a tradition he does not completely understand.

Another element from pagan myth is probably Beowulf's preternatural underwater feats. Rationalistic explanation of some of them simply blinks the fact that the poem operates in a world where human limitations as we know them do not exist. We may point out analogues to the fight with Grendel's dam in which the hero is merely on a ledge behind a waterfall, not in the water. We may explain that, although Beowulf dives down into the mere, the sea cave into which he is dragged has trapped air in it. We can even try to explain the wrestling hold by which Beowulf was able to rip off Grendel's arm. But this is simply to strain at the gnat and swallow the camel. A hero who has the might of thirty men in his handgrip, who can swim for a week in full armor, who can fight underwater with water monsters for a day or so without coming up for air, and who can swim home from Frisia with thirty byrnies would be perfectly capable of staying underwater throughout the fight with Grendel's dam or of ripping off Grendel's arm by sheer brute strength.

Analogues such as that of the troll under the waterfall are later than *Beowulf* and look like attempts at rationalization of older tales. *Beowulf* explains them, not they *Beowulf.* We might as well face the fact that the author of *Beowulf* did not boggle at the marvelous.

A good many early scholars thought that Breca of the swimming match with Beowulf was a sea deity and attempted to equate his name with the modern "breaker," as that of Grendel was thought to mean "grinder." This idea seems to have gone somewhat out of fashion, partly because of the appearance of Breca in *Widsith* as ruler of the Brondings, along with monarchs known to have actually existed. Whatever we think of the etymology, we must, if we reflect, admit that no mere mortal could have played even the losing part in this remarkable contest. The genealogies mix gods and men, and there is no reason to think that *Widsith* is more discriminating than they. On the whole, the assumption of a pagan myth adapted to the author's purpose seems the best explanation of this passage.

It would be interesting to know exactly how the author and his audience accepted these events. Perhaps they would look upon them as they did upon dragons. None of them, probably, would assert that he had seen a dragon himself, just as few modern individuals have seen a sperm whale, but they believed that dragons existed. If they were asked whether they had ever known a man capable of Beowulf's feats, they would probably have admitted that they had not. "But," they might have added, "that was in the good old days when heroes were really heroes."

The Dark Ages do not seem to have drawn the line between the physically possible and the physically impossible, as we attempt to do today. Nor did Christianity do much to reduce credulity. Apocrypha and saints' lives contain marvels beside which those in *Beowulf* seem rather conservative. We should be mistaken if we thought that hearers or readers of *Beowulf* considered it merely a good yarn or accorded it only Coleridge's "willing suspension of disbelief for the moment that constitutes poetic faith." The characters and events of the story, they would doubtless have felt, were not what one would expect in everyday life; neither are earthquakes, tidal waves, or volcanic eruptions. But they do occur.

A very primitive element which appears both in the main plot and in some of the episodes is the uncle-nephew relationship—more specifically, in its origin at least, the relationship of the nephew and his *eam* (maternal uncle). Among some primitive peoples, such as the Polynesians, his mother's brother was a boy's closest male relative. The tragedy of the fight at Finnsburg is heightened by the fact that uncle and nephew, who fell fighting on opposite sides, are placed on the same pyre. In the digression on Sigemund, Fitela, Sigemund's companion in many of his adventures, is his nephew. Beowulf is not only Hygelac's retainer but his nephew as well, and Wiglaf is Beowulf's nephew. The author does not stress these relationships, and may not have been aware of their significance. On the other hand, he may have assumed that the audience would recognize their importance without his emphasizing it.

Above the stratum of myth we find the legendary-historic. The more recent names in the king lists represent real men, but real men as transmuted by the demands of heroic theme and epic lay, which tend to make them considerably larger than life and a good deal better or worse than they actually were—a tendency that some historians believe they observe even in Plutarch. Heremod, about whom we know very little beyond the allusion in *Beowulf,* appears to have been shaped into a sort of Macbeth—a good man gone very wrong indeed. Other figures, such as Sigemund, who appear elsewhere in Germanic legend have been so thoroughly wrapped in myth that the reality, if it ever existed, has disappeared. However, Finn Folcwalding (also known in the genealogies and in the Finnsburg fragment) appears to be an actual monarch whose fate lent itself to poetic treatment.

Except for Beowulf himself, the chief human characters in the central story can be found elsewhere. Hrothgar and Hrothulf appear in Scandinavian king lists as Hroar and Hrolf (or Ralph) Kraka and stand at the shadowy border of legend and history. The Swedish kings of the second half of *Beowulf,* though even more shadowy, doubtless lived and ruled in the fifth and sixth centuries. Ingeld appears with Hrothgar and Hrothulf in *Widsith,* and Alcuin, writing about 800, alludes to a lay or lays about him. Hygelac is vouched for by the Frankish annals and alluded to in the *Liber monstrorum,* in which his skeleton, preserved in Frisia, is said to be that of a man of gigantic stature (this statement has led to speculation that legend has confused Hygelac and Beowulf, but we might also assume that great size was a family characteristic). In other words, we can find all the important characters in *Beowulf* elsewhere in legend or history—except Beowulf himself.

One reason that Hygelac and the Geats do not figure in later Germanic legend may be that after the disaster predicted in the latter part of *Beowulf* the Geats ceased to exist as a tribe and were gradually lost to memory. In his studies of the story of Ingeld, Kemp Malone points out that, although analogues to Heathobardic tales appear in later legend, they are no longer attached to the Bards. He explains this shift by pointing out that the Bards had moved away from the Baltic area and had been forgotten, so that their deeds were attributed to other tribes.[2] Some Beowulf analogues may have a similar history.

A fair number of analogues have been pointed out, though none is very close to the poem. The favorite is Bjarki, the Bear's Son. But when we examine Bjarki, we find that, although he resembles Beowulf in certain respects, he certainly is not Beowulf. A prototype of Bjarki may have contributed something to the idea of Beowulf, just as some lost Germanic demigod may have, but that is all. In fact, when we consider the character of Beowulf, we need to distinguish the folk figure or folk figures (deity, demigod, bear's son, and what you will) who underlie the character from Beowulf the mortal man presented—and perhaps created—by the poet.

As a man, despite his incredible strength, Beowulf knows that he must die and that in each of his adventures he risks defeat. He does not even enjoy the special magical advantages of many characters in later romances. So long as Arthur had Excalibur, he could not be defeated in battle; so long as he wore the scabbard, he could not shed a drop of blood. Beowulf had no such magical guarantees. For victory, he must trust to his good byrnie, his strength, his valor, and the favor that the god of battles sometimes shows to him who fights unflinchingly for the right. Although one cannot say that his strength was as the strength of thirty because his heart was pure, one does get the impression that his high purpose was an important element in the valor without which mere strength would not have prevailed. These are qualities of human hero, not of a humanized deity or nonhuman folk figure.

The author's imperfect grasp of the nature of trolls may lead us to suspect that before it reached him the harrying of Heorot had been put together in some pagan source closer to the native land of the trolls (however the tale originated, it is an interesting example of the insertion of a supernatural tale into the life of a historical character). The blending of elements in the character of Beowulf was probably an even slower and more complicated process, but it is possible that the character of Beowulf is largely a creation of the author— original in the sense that he has shaped his diverse materials into something that is essentially new. However the poem was created, we have a very complex collection of materials frozen into a final form at a fixed point in time, no matter what their later permutations and combinations were to be. Themes, types, and characters in *Beowulf* turn up later in many places. The proto-Beowulf may turn up in Bjarki and other figures, a ballad on the *Beowulf* theme has been collected in America, analogues have been noted in French medieval literature, and so on. But *Beowulf* remains unique—a reflection of the English spirit in the heroic age.

The England of Beowulf

To understand *Beowulf* as fully as possible, one must know the England of the Heptarchy—the seven little kingdoms (more or less) into which Anglian, Saxon, and Jutish territory was divided until all but Wessex and Mercia were destroyed during the First Viking Wars (870-900). Conditions in the England of this time were not unlike those of Denmark under Hrothgar. Nevertheless, *Beowulf* is an English, not a Danish, poem, and English thought had been colored by Christianity since 600.

The central fact underlying English heroic poetry is the war band, the *posse comitatus,* as Tacitus called it. These war bands came to England as the retinues of the princelings who carved out principalities in England, and they remained the center of military and political organization throughout the Heptarchy. The *comitatus* was a voluntary rather than a tribal organization: a warrior could take service under a leader not of his own tribe, and the early leaders of the invasion of England were doubtless more interested in a recruit's ability to pull an oar and swing a sword than in his tribal antecedents. The tribal homogeneity of early bands of invaders has probably been overstressed, though doubtless most bands were chiefly drawn from a single tribe, just as the core of William's army at Hastings was Norman even though he welcomed any footloose rascal who was willing to risk his neck to win an estate. In the same way a Saxon leader was followed mostly by men of his own tribe but had no objection to Angles, Jutes, Danes, Swedes, Frisians, or Franks to swell their numbers. Alfred recruited many Frisians, as shown by the casualty list of the sea fight at Wight in 897.[3]

Once undertaken, the relationship of lord and retainer imposed certain very binding obligations. The lord was responsible for the well-being of his retainers. He must provide them with food and drink in his hall. He gave them arms, horses, jewels, and land. He led them in war and was responsible for their protection as well as that of the rest of his subjects. The retainer's duty was simple but not always easy. He must serve his lord to the death. If a lord was slain, his retainers could honorably survive him only to avenge him. To make peace with his slayer was the ultimate ignominy.

The well-known Cynewulf-Cyneheard episode in *The Anglo-Saxon Chronicle* under the year 755 (possibly based on an epic lay) furnishes a remarkable example of fidelity to this code.[4] Two groups of retainers elected to die fighting against hopeless odds rather than make peace with those responsible for their lords' deaths. Bede tells of the devotion of thane Lilla, who threw his body before King Edwin to protect him from an assassin and thus gave his life to save his master.[5] Not everyone, of course, lived up to these ideals. *Maldon* is built around the contrast between the retainers who flee when Byrhtnoth falls and those who elect to die beside their master's body. A similar contrast appears in the dragon fight in *Beowulf* between Wiglaf and the retainers who run from the conflict. Whether or not the ideal was followed to the bitter letter, it was the core of the warrior code.

The hall was the center of life of the *comitatus*—clubhouse, dining room, and bedroom. Unlike the great hall of later castles, it was a separate building. During the day the leader dined there with his followers. Seating in the hall was probably by rank. In *The Fates of Men,* the harper (scop?)

is represented as sitting "at the feet" of his lord. The band seems to have been divided into the *dugud* (veterans, knights in a later sense) and the *geogud* (recruits or squires). Both these groups seem to have belonged to the officer class *(eorl-cynn)*. Occasionally one finds allusion to *ceorls* (poorer free-men), who may have corresponded roughly to the men-at-arms (enlisted men) of later periods.

The arms provided varied with the period. At the beginning of the Christian era the Germanic peoples regarded wearing body armor as cowardly. Even after they had abandoned that idea, the armament of the ordinary warrior was simple. To judge by grave finds of the Migration Period (ca. 350-550), it usually consisted of a shield, a thrusting spear, one or more throwing spears (angons, Old English *darod'e*), and an all-purpose knife. In these early grave finds swords are so rare that they seem to have belonged only to men of some rank and wealth. The Saxons may have taken their name from *seax* (knife, dagger): the Dagger Men. The word *seax* was used for various weapons, from a rather short knife to a formidable cutlass—a single-edged blade about twenty inches long. It was with some such weapon that Beowulf cut the dragon in two.

The sword (*sweord,* Continental *spatha*) was a straight, double-edged weapon about thirty inches long. The more elegant swords and *seaxes* and their belts and scabbards were beautifully adorned with gold and jewels. Swords of this quality were often treasured heirlooms, and in heroic legend were given names and, as it were, pedigrees. Three such swords, Hrunting, Nægling, and Wiglaf's sword appear in *Beowulf,* and another such sword, unnamed, appears in the Ingeld episode. Nægling also appears in Norse legend.[6]

Since Beowulf is a sword breaker—a hand slayer—swords cannot play the same part in his story as Excalibur in Arthurian legend and Durendal in *Chanson de Roland.* Their place is filled by his splendid byrnie, which saves his life in his struggles with the *nicors* and with Grendel's dam. Although the byrnie has no name, it is referred to as *Hrædlan laf* (heirloom of Hrethel), and obviously has a history. Another artifact with a history is the necklace (torque?) of the Bro(n)sungs compared with that given to Beowulf at Heorot, whose subsequent history is recorded in the poem.

Helmets and coats of mail are almost unknown in English grave finds and must at first have belonged only to the very wealthy. The descriptions of arms in *Beowulf* are plainly anachronistic, and very probably were considered of almost incredible magnificence even in the author's day. Hrothgar's court had a reputation for unparalleled splendor. Apparently his hall is supposed to have been plated on the outside with gold, and his war band would naturally have accoutrements to match this affluence. The leader who accepted a retainer was expected to arm him, and the return of this armor was the first charge on the estate of the retainer after his death.

Generous gifts of jewelry were expected of a leader, and one of the commonest Old English epithets for "king" or "prince" is "ring giver." The splendid jewelry of the Taplow Barrow, in Kent, and Sutton Hoo finds makes the prodigal gifts in *Beowulf* appear less exaggerated than they might seem, though doubtless the poet feels that Hrothgar's court must have set a remarkably high standard in generosity.

Similar gifts were expected of a queen or princess when she appeared in the hall, which she probably did only on special occasions, as when she appeared to greet a distinguished guest. Most of the women's time was spent in the women's quarters *(bur)*, a building or buildings to which the king and probably other members of the court retired at night. Although women held a relatively high place in Germanic society, they played a rather small part in the life of the hall.

Since halls were built of wood, we have little archaeological evidence about their construction. The recently discovered remains of a hall of Alfred's time near Cheddar are those of a rectangular building eighty by twenty feet, built of logs set on end in the ground and chinked with moss, clay, or other suitable materials. The halls seem to have had no chimneys. A hole in the roof placed above a fireplace in the center of the floor carried off some of the smoke. Fires from stray sparks were not uncommon. Like a good deal else in the Middle Ages, a royal court was an odd mixture of splendor and squalor.

To an Englishman of the Heptarchy the joys of the hall— food, drink, the gifts of his lord, the song of the scop, and the fellowship and comparative security of the *comitatus*— represented as much felicity as could be found in a rather grim world. Conversely, the greatest misfortune was separation from the *comitatus* by exile *(wraecsid)* or for other causes. The retainer's feeling for the warmth and brightness of the hall is most strikingly shown in Bede's parable of the sparrow in the well-known tale of the conversion of Edwin of Northumbria. This misery of the exile is expressed by Deor, the scop who has lost his place to another, and— even more poignantly—in *The Wanderer.* Convalescent soldiers who "desert" the cheerless impersonality of a hospital to return to their outfit at the front can probably understand an Anglo-Saxon's feeling for his war band.

By saving Ecgtheow, Beowulf's father, from the wanderings of exile, Hrothgar placed him under deep obligation. The predicted sorrows of the Geats when the Swedes find that Beowulf no longer protects them reflect the plight of the Anglo-Saxon who had lost his lord and his hall.

The principal occupations of a well-born Englishman under the Heptarchy were war and the chase; yet although the chase plays a considerable part in later poetry, such as *Sir*

Gawain and the Green Knight, it is barely mentioned in Old English poetry. War was of various kinds. Before 800, any Viking raids that may have occurred were minor affairs. Kingdoms that still shared a frontier with the Celts tried to enlarge their lands by conquest or to retain what they had won against counterattacks by the Welsh and the Picts. Neighboring kingdoms periodically waged war on each other, singly or in alliance, sometimes with the Celts, as when Mercia allied itself with Cædwal of North Wales against Northumbria. From time to time an English king managed to establish himself as *bretwalda* (king paramount) with a suzerainty over his fellow kings. According to Bede, a special standard *(tufa)* was carried before the *bretwalda* at all times.[7] Just how much authority this position conferred on the holder is not clear—probably as much as he could enforce. If the *bretwalda* died or was defeated in war, his office changed hands or fell vacant until someone else could win it.

Like their Continental cousins, English kings, when they patched up their feuds, often used a royal lady as a sort of seal on the peace treaty. That is, a sister or daughter of one king was married to the other king or to his son. The impression that this system never worked is probably misleading. It was only when it failed, as it frequently did, that it became a subject for the historian or the poet. When the peace broke down, the unfortunate woman found herself torn between two loyalties. Such a situation appears in the story of Finnsburg and in the Ingeld episode.

As if intertribal war were not enough, the little kingdoms were frequently rent by internecine war. Sometimes they split into their earlier components, as Northumbria tended to break down into the two earlier kingdoms Deira and Bernicia. More frequently they engaged in wars of succession. Early English kingship did not automatically pass by primogeniture. Upon the death or—not uncommonly—the deposition of a king, the *witan* (council of magnates) chose as his successor the member of the royal house whom it considered best qualified. Alfred the Great, for example, succeeded his brother Ethelred I, even though Ethelred left two young sons. This method avoided the problems of a long royal minority, but since any prince of the royal house who could raise a strong following could make a push for the throne, the Heptarchy was involved in a whole series of "Wars of the Roses."

In the occasional circumstance that there was no convenient war going on, a quarrelsome atheling could seize the occasion to pursue one of the hereditary blood feuds in which his family was involved or to start a new one by attacking some neighbor who had annoyed him. Killings could be compounded by the payment of *wergeld* (a sum fixed by law according to the rank of a victim), but with such inveterate feudists as the English even this did not guarantee that the feud would not break out again. The stories of Finn and Ingeld deal with intertribal feuds that broke out anew after a peace, and the same thing doubtless happened in interfamily feuds.

Then, too, the *wergeld* was not always offered or accepted. One suspects that in such a society the payment of *wergeld* was considered rather chicken-hearted. Unless a feud was compounded, it was the duty of the family of the latest victim to exact vengeance. The Christian doctrine of forgiveness of enemies found little place in early English thought, and none whatever in *Beowulf.* When King Oswald fell in battle, he prayed for his own soul and those of his men, but he had no prayers to spare for his enemies.[8] After the death of Æschere, Beowulf tells Hrothgar that it is better to avenge a friend than to mourn him too much.

The obligation to vengeance did not seem to be mitigated by the fact that the deceased deserved to be killed. When

102

Grendel's dam seeks vengeance for her son's death, the poet seems to consider her attitude perfectly natural and even legitimate. Twice in *Beowulf* we encounter characters who are caught between two absolutes—the duty of vengeance and the impossibility of exacting it. One is the old man whose son has been hanged for crime; the other is Hrethel, one of whose sons has accidentally killed the other.

It is very difficult for modern readers to recapture the Anglo-Saxon attitude toward war as the natural occupation of a gentleman. The attitude is reflected in the last words of one of the Percys as he lay dying on the battlefield: "And thanks be to God there are but few of my ancestors who have died in their beds." Still earlier it was expressed by Earl Siward of Northumbria (d. 1055) who found himself in some danger of dying of old age and infirmity: "Have I survived so many battles to die like a sick cow?" To such men war was something between a sport and a religion: a way to profit, a path to glory—almost a moral obligation. Hotspur's speech on honor in *Henry IV* is a belated echo of Beowulf's: "It is best for an earl to win lasting fame before death." A Christian might accept the implication of the brevity of life and the fleetingness of earthly joys, but such immortality as glory *(dom)* can confer is hardly a Christian ambition.

The closest modern American parallel to this state of mind is probably that of the professional athlete toward his sport, as revealed, for example, in George Plimpton's *Paper Lion.* Like Beowulf, the athlete is not indifferent to the financial rewards of valor, but the importance of these rewards is in part that they are a measure of that valor. We are told (lines 1025-26) that Beowulf had no need to be ashamed of the gifts of Hrothgar. One might think that if Hrothgar had been niggardly in gift giving he—not Beowulf—should have been ashamed. Yet both the warrior and the athlete might fear that inadequate recompense would cast doubt on the merit of their performance.

Beyond the desire for financial reward, both the warrior and the athlete desire to perform worthily and to win the respect of their fellows and the world at large—in Anglo-Saxon terms to exhibit *ellen* (valor) and to win *dom* (glory). For this they were willing to endure labor, as Gawain wandered freezing through the wilds of the Wirall and the athlete endures the rigors of the training camp. For this they will risk injury, always painful and sometimes crippling.

In our softer age, it is true, the athlete runs slight risk of death, but the medieval attitude toward death differs from ours in a way almost impossible for a modern to grasp. Life in the Middle Ages was much shorter and more uncertain than it is today. One who did not perish by the sword might be taken off at any time by famine or pestilence. If he survived these perils, he must endure an old age unmitigated by modern comforts and the palliatives of modern medical science. Under these circumstances he might regard death in battle as at least the lesser evil.

In view of this attitude, Beowulf's survival to live happily ever afterwards or, in the cynical words of Richard III, "to die a good old man" in the odor of sanctity, surrounded by weeping relatives and with all the consolations of the church, would have been shocking and bathetic anticlimax. Failure to realize this simple fact has led to a good deal of misleading comment on the conclusion of *Beowulf,* which will be dealt with in its proper place.

Old English Poetic Themes

Anglo-Saxon secular poetry was not entirely concerned with battle, murder, and sudden death. We have a few elegies

(The Wanderer, The Seafarer, The Ruin) of considerable poetic quality, laments such as *Deor,* riddles (of which the English seem to have been particularly fond, since they wrote them in both Latin and English), gnomic verses, *Widsith* (a sort of historical miscellany largely concerned with the rulers of various peoples), and some other odds and ends. Of these forms the elegy seems to have influenced *Beowulf,* in lines 2231-70 and elsewhere. The description of the last of a mighty race burying the tribal treasures in the barrow parallels in spirit, and to some extent in content, the reflections on ruined seats of former greatness in *The Wanderer* and *The Ruin.* In its feeling for the brevity of human joy and glory Anglo-Saxon paganism parallels Christian thought. In fact, similar passages can be found in Old English homilies. The conclusions drawn are different, however. The Christian fixes his eyes on the next world; the pagan seeks the immortality of a lasting fame.

There are some gnomic comments in *Beowulf,* usually with the *swa sceal mon don* (so ought a man do) formula to point out some action in the poem as an example of the proper thing, and, in one of Hrothgar's speeches to Beowulf, some moralizing advice not unlike a passage in *The Wanderer* on what a man must undergo to be wise.

On the use of the sea and sailing in *Beowulf,* see "The Formulaic Style of *Beowulf,*" below. On whether the exchange between Beowulf and Unferth may be the development of a theme, see the treatment of this passage in chapter 5, in the discussion of lines 529-606.

Essentially, however, *Beowulf* is a poem of combat, and its themes are the themes of heroic poetry, though it differs from other Old English poetry of its kind in that its important combats are single fights, not battles. A few are battles summarized in the second part, but they are not very fully developed. The central themes of this poetry are the ideals of the *comitatus:* courage, loyalty, and, in the leader, generosity. In *The Fight at Finnsburg* we are told, "Never did retainers better repay the white mead" that they had drunk at their lord's table. In *Maldon* we have a contrast between the disloyal thanes who fled when Byrhtnoth fell and the loyal ones who fought to the death to avenge their master. In *Beowulf* itself we have two such contrasts: that between the retainers who stoically face what they believe to be certain death in Heorot and those who flee from the dragon fight. At the dragon fight itself we have the contrast between the heroic Wiglaf and these cowards.

A concomitant of this loyalty is the *beotword* spoken by the retainer when he receives favors from his lord and promises to repay them on the field of battle or the one spoken by a warrior about to fight or even during a conflict. The customary glossing of this expression as "boastword" or "boastful word" is misleading. It was the proper thing to do: a statement of intention. Once made, it must be lived up to or died by. A later parallel is the "big talk" of men in rough occupations. A cowboy who announced that he could ride anything that wore hair or the lumberjack who stated that he could lick anyone in the crowd might merely be exhibiting *virtus*. Only if he failed to back up his bluff was he regarded as a windy braggart. So in Old English poetry, which is filled with *beotword*. To make one good was the path to honor; to fail to do so or at least to die trying meant disgrace.

The principal virtue of a leader was generosity (the *fredom* of Chaucer's Knight). This generosity appears throughout Old English poetry and demands the passages in which Hrothgar, Wealhtheow, and Hygelac bestow magnificent gifts on Beowulf. Also, no doubt, ambitious young thanes delighted in accounts of the rewards of valor.

Loyalty in a king also demanded that if necessary he die with, or for, his people. Few English kings of this period seem to have saved themselves by flight from a stricken field (in fact, we can think of none before Ethelred the Redeless), but only Beowulf actually sacrifices himself to save his followers.[9]

A special form of loyalty was involved in the blood feud. A man must avenge his kinsman or his lord. Even if the feud had been compounded, one who made peace with the slayer was likely to brood over his shame until, like Hengest at Finnsburg, he broke the peace. Beowulf settles a blood feud for the Danes by slaying Grendel and his dam. He slays Dæghrafn, the slayer of Hygelac. In the second part of the poem, in an episode passed over very lightly, he makes peace with Onela, who was responsible for Heardred's death, but later achieves vengeance by allying himself with Eadgils, another aspirant to the Swedish throne, and thus bringing about the death of Onela. We may assume that the author included this passage only because he considered it a necessary piece of history. Making peace with Heardred's slayer could be justified only as a means of saving the kingdom of the Geats. Whether the poet really approved of Beowulf's vengeance is uncertain, but the vengeance was necessary to save Beowulf's reputation in the eyes of the audience.[10]

Although detailed descriptions of a battle are missing from *Beowulf,* two other elements of the heroic poem appear— the individual combat and the gathering of the carrion eaters, the eagle, the raven, and the wolf. Besides Beowulf's own fights we have the fight at Ravenswood between Ongenthiow and Eofor and Wulf in which Ongenthiow falls. The eagle and the raven appear in the speech of the herald of ill omen who predicts the fate of the Geats now that Beowulf is dead.

Battle poems are full of speeches—*beotword,* exchanges between adversaries, and what the romans called the *exhortatio,* a commander's address to his troops before battle. The two last are missing from *Beowulf* for obvious reasons. His adversaries are not the sort with whom one could carry on a conversation, and we do not see him leading troops into battle. Of *beotword,* however, there are plenty, not only those of Beowulf before each of his contests but also those of Wiglaf before he goes to the aid of Beowulf in the dragon fight. Under the latter circumstances, as in *Maldon,* where these speeches are uttered while the battle is in progress, the *beotword* becomes a rather artificial convention, like the Elizabethan aside. We may doubt whether Wiglaf would have paused to make a rather protracted speech while Beowulf was in dire peril instead of hastening to his aid, but convention demanded such a speech. If we like, we may regard it as a way of presenting Wiglaf's emotions rather than as an actual speech—as what he would have said if he had taken time to say it.

The other speeches in *Beowulf* are probably the result of two things: the poet's interest in courtly behavior, including courtly speech, and the general liking of Anglo-Saxon poets for direct discourse (to judge by the amount of dialogue in the *Edda,* Norse poets shared this liking). The fondness for the exact words of the speaker probably reflects the mental habits of a culture. Even today the narrative of the unlettered runs largely to "I says to him" and "He says to me." Although often tedious, such reporting sometimes attains a vigor and effectiveness hard to achieve by other means.

The *Beowulf* poet obviously was thoroughly familiar with the traditional tales of his people and with the conventional themes and methods of Old English poetry and used them selectively and effectively.

CHAPTER 8

The Versification of *Beowulf*

A NGLO-SAXON versification is, we fear, something of a
mare's nest. This may be an obscurantist view, but it is,
in our opinion, more justifiable than that of the true believer in one or another of the various systems from which
one may choose. Although any sober opinion deserves careful consideration, especially on such a vexed subject, and
any student of Anglo-Saxon poetry should acquaint himself
with the chief scholarship on the subject, it is melancholy
to consider that students should spend a great many hours
each term laboriously committing to memory the intricate
rules established by the theories to which their professors
adhere, in view of the fact that not very many scholars
agree wholly with one another and that some of the foremost
authorities are completely at odds. The fact is that we *know*
very little about either Anglo-Saxon versification or its
rhythm. We know something about what the poet *did,* but
we know next to nothing about the *theory* on which he
based his performance. The details of alliteration are somewhat more firmly established and command a wide degree
of acceptance. This chapter will first make some introductory comments on the verse of *Beowulf* and then give a
sketchy summary of the principal theories of scansion since
1885, followed by a discussion of alliteration, and our own

suggestions for reading the poem. We feel obliged by the nature of our surveylike approach to give an account of the theories about Anglo-Saxon verse. However, the student who has not much need to deal with this aspect of the poem may skip to the section on alliteration.

A few observations about the verse of *Beowulf* may be helpful to the beginning student before our discussion of the various theories of prosody and rhythm. *Beowulf,* like other Anglo-Saxon poems, is composed in verses or half lines, usually of four to seven syllables each. These are printed by most editors in pairs on the same line, the half lines making a long line with a very emphatic division (line 2669):

Æfter ðam wordum   wyrm yrre cwom,

(After these words   the worm fiercely charged,)

Here the sense of the two verses is continuous grammatically, but frequently the verses are almost self-contained syntactic units that allow little or no "run-on" of sense from the first half line to the second. One notes that the verses are bound together by alliteration (*wordum* and *wyrm*) rather than the end rhyme characteristic of later poetry.

The half line and alliteration seem typical of the older Germanic line of poetry, an example of which may be found as far back as the fourth or fifth century in the inscription on the famous golden horn of Gallehus, which runs:

"Ek HlewagastiR HoltijaR / Horna tawido" ("I, Hlewagast, son of Holt, made this horn"). HoltijaR may mean "of Holstein." The inscription may not be a verse, though it appears to be (the golden horn, found in North

Schleswig in the early eighteenth century, was destroyed by a thief in 1802; it has been dated ca. 400).

Terms of description vary, but we call the first half line the "a verse" and the second the "b verse." The verse, with its alliteration, is clearly stress or accentual verse, and we call a primary stressed syllable (like *wyrm* in line 2669) a "lift," and an unstressed one (like the second syllable of Æfter) a "dip." Very frequently syllables appear to receive a secondary stress (like the first syllable of *yrre*), but unfortunately there is no handy term for this, and we shall have to make do with "secondary stress." Many scholars speak also of tertiary stresses and other degrees, but such fine distinctions run a greater-than-usual risk of subjectivity.

Scansion

The most important of the earlier theories of Germanic versification was established by Edouard Sievers in 1885.[1] Sievers combined the obvious facts of stress and alliteration in Germanic verse with a theory of syllabic quantity borrowed from Latin prosody, and evolved his famous ·"Five Types." We should perhaps note here that Latin quantitative scansion is based on the length of syllables whereas qualitative prosody (e.g., Germanic) is based on the stress given to a syllable. A long syllable in Latin, and as Sievers applies it to Anglo-Saxon, is one that contains a long vowel or a diphthong or a short vowel or diphthong "closed" by two immediately succeeding consonants; a short syllable is one that has a short vowel or diphthong left "open" by a single following consonant. Most university texts of *Beowulf* print the Anglo-Saxon with macrons marking the long vowels—

111

we avoid these marks of length except in the brief passage following.

Supported by impressive statistical evidence, Sievers classified nearly all the more than six thousand verses of *Beowulf* into these five patterns, which he named A, B, C, D (with two main varieties), and E. He argued that the lifts, or heavy stresses, in the Anglo-Saxon lines were four only, two to each verse. He divided these lifts and accompanying secondary stresses and unstressed syllables into two measures, or feet, in each verse (half line), and he marked the division in his scansion with a vertical bar.

According to Sievers, the lift falls on the long syllable. Short syllables are normally unstressed or given secondary stresses. Although long syllables normally are lifts or secondary stresses, they are frequently "dips" (unstressed syllables), especially in particles and connectives and the pronouns (*he, me, min,* etc.). A short syllable may receive a stress when it is followed by another unstressed syllable (called a "resolution," e.g., *fela missera,* line 153a, in which the first syllable of *fela,* though containing a short vowel, can receive the stress because of a following short vowel). In practice, however, short syllables very often receive stress regardless of such considerations.

Although Sievers thought that the average duration of time between stresses was roughly equal, his theory was nonisochronous; that is, he held that the measures of the verse need not be equal in their duration and that the time spaces form no definite pattern and so do not constitute part of the metrical or rhythmical structure.

Sievers found that the most common stress pattern in Old English verse was "falling," or, to borrow a classical term, essentially "trochaic." According to Sievers, almost 40 percent of the verses of *Beowulf* consist of a lift alternating with a dip. This verse pattern he calls Type A. In its simplest form A is a pair of falling measures, as in line 10b (we indicate lifts by ´, secondary stresses by ˋ, dips by x.

hyran | scolde: ´ x | ´ x

Type B is essentially the reverse, having two rising measures, thus (line 2262b):

Næs hearpan wyn: x ´ | x ´

Type C is an inversion, a rising measure followed by a falling (line 4a):

Oft Scyld | Scefing: x ´ | ´ x

Sievers's Type D consists of two unequal measures, one of a single lift and another of three syllables consisting of a lift, a secondary stress, and a dip (line 1653a):

leod | Scyldinga: ´ | ´ ˋ x

Another variation of Type D has a different pattern in the second measure line 998a):

eal | inneweard: ´ | ´ x ˋ

Hence one sometimes sees a reference to the "Five [or Six] Types" of Sievers. The last type, E, is essentially a reverse of Type D (line 463b);

Suđ-Dena | folc: ´ ˋ x | ´

Since, however, *Beowulf*'s verses may contain four to ten syllables (not counting the "hypermetric lines"),[2] it is obvious that these patterns, which in their basic form allow for four to six syllables, will not by themselves account for nearly all the verses of the poem. In addition to "resolution," two or more unstressed syllables may be allowed in varying positions in the patterns. Also, of course, the device of anacrusis allows Sievers to consider unstressed syllables preceding the first lift of the first measure as extrametrical (e.g., line 1248a, "ge æt ham ge on herge"), in which the first two syllables are described as "extrametrical prelude, and hence a Type A emerges:

$$x\,x\,\|\,\acute{}\,x\,x\,|\,\acute{}\,x$$

In sum, the Five Types are expanded to include many, many subtypes and variations. Although in practice Sievers's system is complicated, his principles are clear: (1) the verse of Anglo-Saxon poetry contains two main lifts and one or more dips, composing two feet or measures a verse; (2) the quantity of syllables bears a direct relationship to the distribution of lifts and dips; (3) the measures are nonisochronous; and (4) the five types are independent; that is, each exists as an entity and is not simply a variation of the most common type, A.

Several criticisms have been made of Sievers's system, the most important of which are these: (1) the rigidity of reading, which led him frequently to assign lifts and dips and bars where few others would agree, with the result that the system and a rational rhetorical reading of the lines sometimes bear no relation to one another; (2) his use of Latin syllabic quantity; and (3) his failure to take into consideration the time of a verse, so that his D and E verses

114

in particular make for very awkward reading. The first objection is discussed below in connection with A. J. Bliss's elaborations on the Sievers system, and the third is the basis of the criticism of Heusler, John C. Pope, and others, which is taken up in its turn. Sievers's use of syllabic quantity has not been challenged as much as it might be. Only Paull F. Baum has given careful attention to it.[3] He points out that we know very little indeed of Anglo-Saxon syllabic quantity and should not without question adopt features of Latin versification for a language that in so very many ways differed from Latin. Our knowledge of the Anglo-Saxon vowel quantity is derived from what we can trace of sound changes and analogies with other Germanic languages and to some extent is also based on metrical evidence. If this metrical evidence is founded in part on a scansion assuming syllabic quantity, then at least some of the argument is inevitably circular. We do not suggest that syllabic quantity played no part in Anglo-Saxon versification but agree with Baum that no really convincing review of the whole problem has been made.

Max Kaluza refined Sievers's system in several ways.[4] He relentlessly tracked down the subvarieties of the Five Types and classified many as individual types, producing ninety types in all. His system was clearly cumbersome and has never been widely adopted. He also suggested the function of a "rest" in the line as a buffer between verses and so in a sense anticipated some of the work of Heusler and Pope, of the isochronous school, who have made great use of the musical concept of the rest.

Bliss's study of 1958 is the most important that has been done in the tradition of Sievers.[5] It is an enormously impressive statistical documentation, in which each verse of *Beowulf* receives careful classification. Although in the main Bliss regards his study as a confirmation of Sievers's principles, he differs from the earlier scholar in important ways and has approached Sievers's work with a critical mind. Bliss's work was supplemented in 1962 by a pamphlet, *An Introduction to Old English Metre,* which eliminated the argumentation of the main work and made its principles much more accessible to the student.

Briefly, Bliss maintains the soundness of Sievers's Five (or Six) Types and demonstrates that they are the basic variations that the language allows on the underlying Anglo-Saxon pattern of falling rhythm in two measures, or "breath-groups," as Bliss calls them. He goes on to concede the rigidity of certain features of Sievers's classification and concludes that the Anglo-Saxon verse, far from being invariably a two-lift verse, in fact frequently allowed either one or three lifts. He also, in a chapter remarkable for its brevity and lucidity (chapter 5), revises Sievers's theory of the dividing bar and makes it a more meaningful caesura separating the breath-groups, that is, the group of words in a verse that one would speak as a group, in a single breath (not that Bliss conceives of the scop as having gasped for air in the middle of each verse). Bliss thus allows for a verse with three lifts, which he calls "heavy," and a single lift, which he calls "light," but then insists on squeezing them into the two-measure verse patterns of Sievers; hence the third lift in the "heavy" verse must become secondary, and the "light" verses are treated as having "suppressed" stresses.

Bliss worked out a much more elaborate system of classification than Sievers's and, given its frame of reference, a much more accurate one. In addition to the broad classification of Sievers's types and such special categories as "light" verses, which are designated in lower-case type, there are many number-and-letter combinations together with asterisks and pluses, so that a verse may be designated by as many as five symbols. Clearly such a system has its limitations for students.

Thus far we have been dealing with scholars in the tradition of Sievers, which we may call the non-isochronous school. Sievers himself, however, came to doubt part of his earlier theory and in 1925 published a study in which he apparently came round to argue that the measures were of equal duration and thus converted to the doctrine of isochronous analysis.[6]

In the same year, Andreas Heusler published his *Deutsche Versgeschichte.*[7] In it he proposed a method of reading Germanic and Anglo-Saxon verse that kept time, the two measures of each verse being of equal duration. Heusler invented his own method of assigning time to the syllables according to a musical analogy of 4/4 time. But since he held basically to Sievers's analysis of the five patterns of stress, considering them five ways of filling a musical line, he was hard put to make the measures come out even without grotesque exaggeration. To help overcome this difficulty, he borrowed another device from music, the rest, and with it "filled out" measures that were obviously not of equal duration with others, particularly in Sievers's D and E types, which assign one whole measure to a major lift.

Heusler's system was greatly elaborated in 1942 by J. C. Pope, who detailed a system of analysis that is now widely accepted in the United States and to some extent in Europe.[8] Pope used the symbols of musical notation to indicate duration of time (4/8 instead of Heusler's 4/4, which removed some of Heusler's exaggeration) and, deeply influenced by William Thomson's theories,[9] essentially denied the rising or "iambic" rhythm patterns to Anglo-Saxon verse (in Heusler's theory this is a result of his describing all syllables before the initial stress as anacrusis). Instead of Sievers's rising patterns in Type B and the first foot of Type C, Pope postulates a stressed rest for the first heavy stress (line 4a):

Type C: Oft Scyld Scefing

Sievers: x ⌣ | ⌣ x

Pope: (⌣) 𝅗 | 𝅘 𝅗 x

Thus by assigning a quarter rest (an initial stress in parentheses) before the verse begins, he is able to achieve the equivalent of a half note in the first measure, matching the duration of the quarter and two eighth notes of the second measure. The result is that the rising rhythm of Sievers's notation is reversed and something like a Sievers Type D emerges. Because of the widespread use of Sievers's type classification, Pope keeps essentially to the old letter labels.

Realizing the tenuous nature of a stressed rest, Pope developed his theory of the use of the harp as accompaniment. He conceived of a harp stroke frequently occupying the time space of the rest and serving as the invisible stress at the beginnings of those verses that his theory of notation required to have a stressed rest. Pope recognized his problem clearly: "Initial rests are easy enough to produce and to hear so long as another verse precedes them. They cannot be produced, on the other hand, at the beginning of a poem, or after a considerable pause in the midst of it, unless some external means of marking the position of the latent accent is employed."[10]

The external means of marking the latent stress, then, was the harp. It is perhaps incorrect to regard the use of the harp as the foundation of Pope's theory of rhythm, as some opponents have seemed to do; the postulation merely solves some technical problems and, if accepted, makes the larger isochronous theory more convincing. Nor does the isochronous theory make less important the function of the lifts and dips in the verse.

There are, however, several difficulties with Pope's theory. Some difficulties inhere in any theory that attempts both exactness and comprehensiveness, and the weakness of subjectivity from which Sievers suffered is shared by Pope. In insisting upon equal duration of measures everywhere, Pope runs afoul of common sense, as in such a simple line as 529:

> Beowulf mapelode,   bearn Ecgpeowes:

Pope assigns a quarter note to each of the two syllables of *Beowulf* and an eighth note to each of the syllables of *mapelode.* There is not much to quarrel with here, though one is tempted to object that surely the second and last syllables of *mapelode* are not equivalent to the first and third. But in the second verse, *bearn* is given a half note, the first syllable of *Ecgpeowes* a quarter, and the other two syllables an eighth note apiece. The two words are thus musically equivalent. This is simply not true. *Ecgpeowes* is not a group of throwaway syllables; not only is it rhetorically at least as important as *bearn,* but the first two syllables are long, by the usual definition. Any but a comic reading must give *Ecgpeowes* more *time* than *bearn.* Since the phrase is an epithet, a rest cannot be urged to extend *bearn,* for it would break up the unit. A by-now-famous example used to object to Pope's system is *wis welpungen* (line 1927a), a verse of Sievers's Type D. Pope assigns the same time to the two words, evening the balance by positing a quarter rest after *wis:*

,

119

wis *ı* | welþungen

Bliss has argued that such a reading breaks up the sense of the verse.[11] Even if one concedes a pause between coordinate adjectives, Pope's analysis remains difficult to accept. One can find many similar readings to quarrel with in the courageously complete catalogue given by Pope in his appendix.

Of course, the principle of the rest seems built into the Anglo-Saxon verse in the scheme of line division, the half line. There is little more enjambment between the lines themselves than between the verses, and so there is always ample space for the rhetorical rest to achieve balance and emphasis, and any recitation of the poem makes full use of this. The difficulty with Pope's analyses is simply that the case for a strictly isochronous reading of the measures of the verse is not an overwhelming one. If one grants that it probably was isochronous, then, by the judicious use of rests and rigorous assignment of time to syllables, one can make most of the verses support such a case. But the initial case is weak. We have no way of knowing, first, whether Anglo-Saxon verse was musically conceived or constructed and, second, whether, if it was, the musical framework was isochronous. We have no English musical notation before the eleventh century. We have reconstructed an Anglo-Saxon harp (several times) but have no sure knowledge of how it was strung or played. The English folk song has a strong nonisochronous tradition. And the only music that existed in England during the Anglo-Saxon period of which we have any reasonable knowledge was nonisochronous Gregorian chant. Pope, in the preface to the reprint of his book in 1966, is positively discourteous to Paull Baum, who had called attention to these facts,[12] and completely distorts Baum's argument. Pope argues that we have no evidence that Gregorian chant influenced Anglo-Saxon poetry.[13] That is not, of course, what Baum had suggested. Baum had simply asked why, since the only music in England in this period of which we know anything was *non*isochronous, should we *assume* that Anglo-Saxon music and poetry *were* isochronous? This should appear to any unprejudiced mind a considerable argument.

Pope's harp also presents problems. One understands the appeal of the harp as the marker or baton to "strike" the stressed rest, which otherwise would be indistinguishable from any other variety of silence; but, again, in spite of Pope's confidence, the evidence of harp accompaniment to Anglo-Saxon verse is contradictory. There are allusions in *Widsith* and elsewhere, including *Beowulf,* which lend themselves to the interpretation that the harp accompanied the chanting of poetry; there are other references which seem to suggest that they were different activities.[14] And even if the harp was played during the oral performance of poetry, as we may say it likely was, at least on occasion, why must we assume that it was used as Pope suggested? It may have been used for prelude or postlude or to emphasize the rhetorically important phrases, or it may have accompanied in something of a modern sense, keeping up a rhythmic variation. It would seem improbable that an instrument of several strings and presumably capable of some variation would have been used primarily to mark rests when the femur of a deer thumped on a table would have served equally well.

We are also unconvinced by Pope's thesis that Anglo-Saxon verse possessed no rising rhythm. It is not impressive to dispose of the many examples of Sievers's B and C verses by the expedient of positing an initial stressed rest that inverts the pattern. Since the concept of a stressed rest is itself a questionable assumption and since the many examples of rising rhythm are reasonably physical, we prefer to continue to recognize them until they are explained away more convincingly.

In addition to the challenges of Bliss and Baum, there have been other attacks on the isochronous school. One of the most impressive is a short article by Josef Taglicht, which with admirable conciseness puts the case against Pope, as well as against Sievers and Bliss.[15] Taglicht suggests in his turn a chronometric analysis, which is based upon syllabic length rather than temporal duration; unfortunately Taglicht has more success for the prosecution than for the defense, and his proposal has not been widely accepted.

Baum not only attacks the two main theories but presents his own suggestions for an interpretation of Anglo-Saxon verse. According to Baum, we are freed from many logical difficulties if we accept the "falling" or "trochaic" rhythm of the verse as the basic rhythm that sets the "tune" of the verse (Sievers classifies about 40 percent of the verses as Type A) and recognize the other patterns as variations like those with which Milton or Shakespeare varied the rhythm of his lines against the counterpoint of the steady underlying iambic beat of blank verse. This theory of counterpoint is not new, and there is a sense in which it was accepted by both Sievers and Pope. Baum argues that, although the variations do fit chiefly into Sievers's types, yet those types themselves have almost endless subtypes (cf. Kaluza's ninety types and Bliss's and Pope's infinite varieties). To attempt to nail them all down would be as pointless as to catalogue the varieties of rhythm in *Paradise Lost* or *Hamlet* whenever there is not regular iambic pentameter. Although Pope dismisses Baum's view as "loosely conceived,"[16] there is much that recommends Baum's flexibility and his freedom from tiresome dogma. Baum reads *Beowulf* much as any other person reasonably familiar with the sound and meaning of the language and the rhetorical emphases of the verse might do; there is no straining of syllables to take up more than a reasonable amount of time, nor the portentous rests that mar in practice the theories of the isochronous school. But Baum's view appears to have fallen into the void.

In 1966, Robert P. Creed presented a much simplified and in some ways radically different version of Pope's system.[17] To the scholar who is predisposed to accept the isochronous theory and is not unnerved by the idea of students carefully marking rests and harp strokes to achieve the isochronous structure, Creed's system is unquestionably an advance on Pope's in both consistency and usability.

John Nist has an intriguing approach that combines a rough isochronism with a theory of percussional harp substitution, and the result is a syncopated, rather jazzy poem.[18] He finds sixteen basic cadences in the verses and recognizes only three degrees of stress as compared with Pope's five. Each cadence begins with a primary stress that is normally signaled by the alliteration of the line (syllables in anacrusis are not, of course, counted). The alliteration produces an overemphasis, with the result that normal secondary stresses become primary, and tertiary stresses become secondary. Nist argues that "this introduction of secondary accents into the measures of *Beowulf* is automatically accompanied by open junctures, which substitute for missing tertiary stresses."[19] The poem is marked by open junctures between primary syllables, and these were filled, Nist believes, by a percussive harp stroke. This makes it unnecessary to distort a syllable by prolongation to fill out a measure. For instance, in *bat ban-locan* (line 742a), Nist would use a harp stroke between the contiguous primary stresses of *bat* and *ban,* with the result that *bat* plus harp stroke roughly equals *ban-locan.* A harp chord, he explains, "substitutes for the missing secondary stress . . . in the same manner in which open junc-

ture . . . substitutes for missing tertiary stress."[20] The pos-
tulated harp stroke does not, of course, appear in every verse,
but it is involved in eight of the sixteen cadence patterns
discerned by Nist. Nist gives an example not of his cadences
but of his idea of the harp's use in the first three lines of
Beowulf (harp stroke represented by H):

Hwæt! we Gar-[H]Dena   in gear-[H]dagum,
þeod-[H]cyninga   þrym [H] gefrunon,
hu ða æþelingas   ellen fremedon.[21]

Nist makes generally good sense, once one concedes the
probability that the harp was used in the way that Nist describes. But there is no concrete evidence for the theory.
Nist argues that the harp is the key to analysis of Anglo-
Saxon verse. One can only answer, Perhaps so, but then
again, perhaps not. At any rate, Nist's *Beowulf* is certainly
entertaining.

In drawing to an end this review of scholarship's attempts
to recover Anglo-Saxon prosody and rhythm, we must conclude that no system has yet found universal acceptance
and that even Sievers's famed Five Types must be recognized as no more than a description of stress distribution,
in spite of Bliss's attempt to reestablish them as a complete
accounting. One concludes that the very complication of
Bliss's and Pope's systems militates strongly against their
genuine utility to the student. It may be that one or the
other is 100 percent correct, but only a guarantee of such
accuracy would justify the labor necessary to master and
apply the details of the systems. Creed, Baum, and Nist have
in their favor a relative simplicity, and the operation of
Occam's razor would seem to recommend one of them if
the reader feels obliged to adhere to a system.

On the whole, extremely complicated theories of Old English versification seem to overlook such facts as we possess about the composition of poetry in the period. If Caedmon and his fellow herdsmen and plowboys could be expected to compose verse extemporaneously at a feast, we cannot assume that poetry was the exclusive property of a special class of bards and must, on the other hand, assume a technique that could be rather easily mastered, very likely by ear: by hearing verse patterns and reproducing them (otherwise, the miracle of Caedmon's song takes on an added dimension). Today, for example, a person with a reasonably good ear who has heard enough ballads can compose a ballad and stay within the bounds of permissible variation with no formal knowledge of prosody. Professional scops doubtless developed various tricks of the trade, which they passed on to their apprentices, but to assume an elaborate Old English *Ars poetica* seems to us to be going considerably beyond the evidence.

Alliteration

On the main questions of alliteration most students have been in rough agreement. We are guided by alliteration in assigning the basic lifts of the verse, and, in our reading, the other lifts and dips have fallen into place around the alliteration. This is true of Pope and the isochronous school as well as of Sievers and Bliss, though not to the same degree, since the former hear silent lifts as well. Over the years a theory of distribution of the alliterative syllables has grown up, the basic principles of which are as follows: (1) initial consonants alliterate with one another, and certain consonant clusters that form a single sound must alliterate as a group, e.g., *sc, st, sp,* which apparently never alliterate with a single *s* (other consonant groups may alliterate on the initial consonant, as *h* and *hr, w* and *wr, s* and *sr,* and so on); (2) initial vowels and diphthongs alliterate with any other initial vowels or diphthongs, e.g., the æ of *æpelingas* with *e* of *ellen* in "hu ða æþelingas   ellen fremedon" (line 3); (3) prefixes do not normally alliterate (except for those that dominate meaning, like *un*), though one is tempted to see extra ornamentation in two or three *ge-* participles or verbs in a line; (4) the most common pattern of alliteration calls for two in the a verse and one in the b verse, though there are many variations; (5) the first lift of the b verse normally falls on a syllable that shares in the alliterative pattern of the line, and hence this syllable is described as the "key" to the alliteration, or "head stave" (German Hauptstab).

As we have said, the most common alliterative pattern is two in the a verse and one in the b verse, or, as we designate it, *a a   a x,* the *x* representing the fourth stressed syllable, which does not alliterate with the other three; e.g., line 1591 (letters representing alliterative sounds are in italic):

*S*ona pæt ge*s*awon   *s*nottre ceorlas
a   *a*   *a*   *x*

and line 1558:

*ea*ldsweord *eo*tenisc   *ec*gum pyhtig
a   *a*   *a*   *x*

The second most common pattern is that of a single alliteration in each verse, or *a x   a y;* e.g., line 360:

Wulfgar maðelode   to his *w*inedrihtne

a   *x*   *a*   *y*

and line 196:

se wæs *m*oncynnes   *m*ægenes strengest

a   *x*   *a*   *y*

These two patterns together account for about 70 percent of the lines in *Beowulf.*

In discussing alliterative patterns other than these two, one encounters considerable confusion and disagreement, partly because the other patterns frequently involve secondary stresses and consequently the question of whether alliteration was intended by the poet. For instance, Baum thinks that 10 percent or more of *Beowulf*'s lines are of the pattern *xa ay*, whereas Pope almost denies their existence.[22] But surely such lines as 28 and 38,

hi hyne þa ætbæron   to *b*rimes farod'e

ne hyrde ic *c*ymlicor   *c*eol gegyrwan

plucked from the first fifty of the poem, must represent some such pattern, though a case might be made that these are verses containing a single lift each (in fact, Bliss classifies the a verse of each of these lines as a "light," or single-lift, verse). At any rate, the *xa ay* pattern exists, and there are many examples.

Several other curiosities in alliterative patterns have perplexed scholars for years. We do not seem to know what to say about transverse alliteration, which might be described as *a b*   *a b.* Baum claims to have found about eighty examples in the poem—not a great many, but enough to throw some doubt on the efforts of Sievers and others to dismiss them as unintentional.[23] Some striking candidates cited by Baum are lines 88 and 39:

> þæt he *d*ogora ge*h*wam   *d*ream ge*h*yrde
>
> *h*ildewæpnum   ond *h*ead'owædum

Perhaps these are accidental, but O. F. Emerson and others made a good case for the existence of such patterns in early Germanic poetry generally.[24] There are other multiple alliterations as well, as in lines 1594 and 236:

> *b*rim *b*lode *f*ah.   *B*londen*f*eaxe,
>
> *m*aegen*w*udu *m*undum,   *m*eþel*w*ordum fraegn:

Such examples Baum calls "secondary alliteration," and the term seems to fit, for the syllables containing the *f*'s in line 1594 and *w*'s in line 236 are clearly secondary lifts. Although the function of these secondary alliterations may be debatable, it would seem difficult to deny that they are there, and equally difficult to conceive that the scop was unaware of them, particularly in lines 131, 208, 209, 1143, 2510, and 2907, as well as in the lines quoted.

Other oddities abound—for example, triple alliteration in the a verse, as in lines 743, 2316, and 2767 and six or seven more, many of them classified by Bliss as "heavy" verses, that is, verses having three lifts instead of two.

Students frequently note that alliteration may appear in "bunches" with one or two dominant sounds in a passage

128

of several lines, and occurring in "run-on" patterns from one line to another. Examples can be found here and there throughout *Beowulf.* A good illustration is lines 760-64:

> ond him *f*æste *wid*l*f*eng;   *f*ingras burston;
> *eo*ten *w*æs *utw*eard,   *eo*rl *f*urþur stop.
> *M*ynte se *m*æra,   (þ)ær he *m*eahte swa,
> *w*idre ge*w*indan   ond on *w*eg þanon
> *f*leon on *f*enhopu;   *w*iste his *f*ingra ge*w*eald

Here the interplay of *f* and *w* separated by a line of vocalic and one of *m* alliterations seems clearly to form a crossing sound pattern between lines 760-61 and 763-64, even when we take into consideration line 762 and the fact that the alliterative pattern of line 761 is vocalic (*eoten* and *eorl*) rather than consonantal and that the two *w*'s in the line are secondary stresses.

End rhyme does occur between verses in *Beowulf,* but it is sufficiently rare (e.g., lines 726, 734, 1014, 2258, and 3172) that it would seem fair to describe it as, if not accidental, then probably the result of a momentary playing with sound by the scop. It does not, at any rate, seem to be functional.

Suggestions on Reading Beowulf

Since we have argued that, although a knowledge of the various theories of meter and rhythm in Anglo-Saxon verse is useful, it would be unfortunate for a student to devote a great amount of time to their study in light of the present state of knowledge, we should perhaps conclude with some simplified suggestions of our own. We seriously doubt that anyone could at this time say anything that had not been said before, at least in part, and all the observations that follow have been offered at various times by others.

Initially, we believe that far too much has been made of the "measure," or, as Bliss calls it, the "breath group," into which the Anglo-Saxon verse is supposedly divided. Although it is possible to draw bars with Sievers and Pope, and although many verses have clear caesuras and the rhythm is generally dipodic, it seems to us that the strict principles of division used by both Sievers and Pope have no demonstrable basis in reality. It seems to us more practical to regard the verse rather than the measure as the basic unit and to consider the verses to be roughly equal in time to their matching verses. We say "roughly" because some are certainly not of the same duration as others,[25] and in any case we do not see that a strictly isochronous analysis solves any of the problems that arise. We do, however, recognize the consistency with which the poet has balanced the verse pairs. Frequently the verses are balanced very closely indeed with one another, each containing the same number of syllables and lifts, as in lines 614, 664, and 2315:

> grette goldhroden   guman on healle
> wolde wigfruma   Wealhþeo secan
> lad lyftfloga   læfan wolde.

Much more frequently, however, a short a verse will have the slack taken up by a long b verse, and vice versa. Almost invariably the longer verse will have fewer or less emphatic lifts to make up for its greater number of syllables, with the result that, with proper rhetorical attention to the lifts by the reader, the verses balance, as in lines 733-34:

> lif wið lice,   þa him alumpen wæs
> wistfylle wen.   Ne wæs þæt wyrd þa gen,

The immediately following two lines (735-36) reverse the pattern:

> þaet he ma moste   manna cynnes
> ðicgean ofer þa niht.   Pryðswyð beheold

As we observed earlier, Anglo-Saxon poetry has in the half-line structure a built-in rest whenever the poet wishes to use it; or, in the beginning of a sentence, as in line 734b above, the rhetorical period ending in line 734a may be taken to make the shorter a verse equal the longer b verse.

Within this normal balance of the verses the scop's aim seems to have been to achieve variation. Only a few lines in the poem have nearly identical verses in the distribution of lifts and dips. Even as rough an analysis as that provided by Sievers's Five Types reveals how frequently the scop reverses the order of lift and dip from one verse to its companion, particularly in matching a shorter A, B, or C type to a D or E type. See the types of the first twenty-five lines as given by Klaeber or, quite fully, the entire census of the verses in Bliss.[26]

The scop, however, sometimes eschews balance for rhetorical effect, as in those verses that, acting as summary or commentary on preceding material, are drawn out of proportion to their paired verses. Here the very imbalance seems a deliberate stylistic effect of the poet, who achieves emphasis by variation on balance, as for example, line 359:

> Deniga frean;   cuþe he duguðe þeaw.

The practice of balancing verse against verse (or block against block, as J. R. R. Tolkien puts it)[27] is made easy by the rhetorical and grammatical structure of the language. The poem moves not by the line but by the verse, and all critics have commented on the building-block style of Anglo-Saxon poetry. Although a straight subject-verb-object progression from one verse to another is not uncommon in *Beowulf,* far more typical is the balancing act seen in the following passage (lines 350b–55):

"Ic þæs wine Deniga,

frean Scildinga   frinan wille,

beaga bryttan,   swa þu bena eart,

þeoden mærne   ymb þinne sid,

ond þe þa andsware   ædre gecydan,

de me se goda   agifan penced."

(I will acquaint the friend of the Danes—the lord of the Scyldings, the giver of bracelets, that famous prince —of this matter about your journey, as you request, and I will return to you the answer that the noble one is pleased to give me.)

Here the clause begins in the b verse, and the operative parts of the sentence follow it also in the b verses; the a verses for three lines are simply variant formula modifiers of *wine* in line 350b; with the conclusion of the opening clause in 353b the new clause begins in the following a and from there proceeds in ordinary "prose" order. The effect in the a verses of lines 351, 352, 353 is to lump the brief formulas in succession, balanced in each instance by the somewhat looser (though not necessarily shorter) patterns in the b verses through which move the grammatically operative parts of the sentence. More on the structure of the verses will be found in our remarks on rhetoric and style in chapter 9.

In summarizing our remarks on balance and time relationship between the half lines, we would repeat that generally the verses of the poem are roughly even, particularly if one makes any effort at proper rhetorical emphases. The alliterative patterns clearly supply the key to the lifts in the verses. We have discussed the varying number of alliterating syllables that a line may contain, but there are at least two recognizable alliterations in a line. These, except for secondary alliterations, always take the heavy stresses of the reading. If there is doubt about which is secondary and which primary, the first lift of the b verse normally, though not invariably, identifies the primary alliterative pattern.

As for those lifts which are not alliterative in their initial syllables, a good guide is a grammatical one, that is, nouns, adjectives, verbs (finite followed by infinitive), and adverbs in descending order of importance. But the clearest aid of all is supplied by simply understanding what the words mean. The *Beowulf* poet, as we have urged, was not a fool, and we may trust him to have intended the rhythmical and metrical emphases to fall generally on important words.

As we have observed, we can normally look for two lifts in each verse, but we must be prepared to read sensibly and see only one when there is only one and three when there are three. Let us examine a passage of a reasonably varied and highly rhetorical nature (line numbers appear at the left for ease of reference):

1383   Beówulf mápĕlŏdĕ,   beárn Ećgpĕowĕs:

1384   "Nĕ sórgă, snótŏr gúmă!   Sélrĕ bĭd' ăˇghwăˇm

133

1385 p̽ǽt hĕ̽ hĭ̽s fréond wrécĕ,   pŏ̃nne hĕ̽ félắ múrnĕ̃.

1386 Úrĕ̃ ǽghwy̆̃lc scĕ́al   éndĕ̽ gĕ̃bídắn

1387 wóröldĕ̃ lífĕ̃s;   wýrcĕ̃ sĕ̃ pĕ̃ mótĕ̃

1388 dómĕ̃s ằr deápĕ̃;   pằt bĭ̆d' dríhtgừmằn

1389 únlĭ̃fgĕ̃ndŭ̃m   ǽftĕ̆r sélĕ̆st.

1390 Ắrís, rícĕ̃s weárd,   ừtŏ̃n hrápĕ̃ férằn,

1391 Gréndlĕ̃s mágằn   gáng scĕ́awĭ̃gằn.

1392 Ìc hằt pè gĕ̃hátĕ̃:   nò hè ŏ̃n hélm lósằp,

1393 nè ŏ̃n fóldằn fắpm,   nè ŏ̃n fýrgĕ̃nhólt,

1394 nè ŏ̃n gýfĕ̃nĕ̃s grúnd,   gá pằr hè wíllĕ̃!"

(Beowulf spoke, son of Ecgetheow: "Sorrow not, wise man! It is better for each man that he avenge his friend, than that he mourn much. Each of us must await an end of worldly life; he who may must work his glory before death; that is to the unliving warrior afterward best. Arise, guardian of the kingdom, let us quickly go out to view the track of Grendel's kin. I promise you this: he will not lose himself in hiding, neither in the bosom of the earth, nor in the fastness of the mountain wood, nor in the bottom of the sea, go where he will!")

In marking the lifts and secondary stresses and eschewing consideration of long and short syllables, we have been guided primarily by the rhetoric and grammar. Although some verses, such as 1394b, thus defy Sievers and Pope because of the emphasis we believe they achieve and require, it is clear that, roughly, our marking does no real violence to Sievers's classification of the five basic patterns of stress in Anglo-Saxon verse. It could not be otherwise, for no one has denied that Sievers did, in fact, describe the basic distribution of stress. Again, the verses as we read them appear to correspond roughly to their partners in time. The steady, falling rhythm of Anglo-Saxon verse dominates beneath an imaginative variation of stress patterns. No verse repeats exactly the meter and rhythm of its partner, except those of line 1393. In a strict application of Sievers's metrical description, several of our markings would have to be changed, of course; for instance, the secondary stresses on the negatives of lines 1392b-1394a would have to go. But this is the failure of strict application of any analysis; here these linking, rhetorically significant adverbs must be emphasized, or what is the speech about? This grimly determined reiteration cannot be masked by an academic refusal to stress Beowulf's *no, ne, ne, ne,* which culminate in the truly epic sealing of Grendel's fate: "ga þaer he wille!" And, surely, in line 1384a, the magisterial "ne sorga, snotor guma" cannot be compressed into the same time space as, for example, "æfter selest." The three commanding primary stresses (and surely *ne* cannot be a "dip" as we normally think of that term) cut short the lament of Hrothgar and sweep into the heroic credo that follows. Likewise with the pronouns of lines 1392-94; in line 1392a, Beowulf is beginning a grimly heroic boast. The poet lines up three pronouns in a row; since pronouns come low on the totem pole in matters of stress, we would be left with a single lift in the line by sticking strictly to Sievers's system: *geháte.* But these are not ordinary pronouns. Beowulf is saying, "I . . . promise . . . you . . . this." We are speaking of *reading* the verse, not scanning it. But as with modern iambic pentameter of good quality, the rhetorical effect of the verse is heightened by our realization that words of slight metrical weight are here being given great weight; our attention is fixed on them by the very irregularity of the arrangement. We have a choice

135

of pattering rapidly up to the stress of *gehate* and banging heavily on the second syllable or of making sense of the line. In the respect that Pope's system allows by its nature an emphasis on the time of the phrasing, it is in some measure superior to Sievers-Bliss.

To summarize: Our advice to anyone approaching *Beowulf* in the original, who wishes to recite it (the only way in which, we feel, the grand old poem can be really appreciated), is that he should master the meanings of the words, key on the alliteration, and let the chips fall where they may. Sievers, Bliss, and Pope, to the extent that their theories are valid, will be done no grave injustice in the result.

CHAPTER 9

The Formulaic Style of *Beowulf*

The student of Old English poetry will no doubt have re-
marked the popularity during the past twenty years of
"oral-formulaic" studies, especially among American scholars. Beginning with F. P. Magoun's famous article in 1953,[1]
a growing body of scholarship has attempted to prove that
much of Old English poetry, including *Beowulf,* was composed orally, extemporaneously, from the traditional stock
of formulas with which the scop was provided in his word
hoard, or poetic vocabulary. The case for oral composition is,
at best, not proven. In our opinion it is most improbable
that *Beowulf* was composed orally, even in smaller units,
but a scrupulous analysis of the evidence is beyond our
scope here.[2] There can be no doubt, however, that the controversy has been helpful in calling renewed attention of
students to the technical characteristics of *Beowulf.* That the
poem is formulaic—i.e., constructed of traditional epithets
and phrases that must have had their origin in a poetry orally composed and transmitted—is obvious. An appreciation of how the formulaic materials are used in Old English
poetry is of the first importance to the reader who wishes to
deal with *Beowulf* in its original language, or even in a competent modern version.

Our discussion has two parts. First, we survey the formulaic material used by Old English poets, and, second, we consider the peculiar characteristics of the kind of poetry that the formulaic tradition produced.

The Epithet and Modifying Formula

The formulaic materials may usefully be considered in four groupings: (1) the epithet and brief modifying formula, (2) the sentence formula, (3) the larger rhetorical patterns that employ formulas in their construction, and (4) the formulaic elaboration of themes.

One kind of epithet, the kenning, is the best known of the formulas.[3] It is a condensed metaphor or simile, for example, "hron-rad" (whale road) for the sea, "sund-wudu" (sea wood) for a ship, "isern-scur" (iron shower) for a flight of arrows, "hildegicelum" (battle icicle) for a sword, and "hæd stapa" (heath stepper) for a deer. Other noun epithets verge on the kenning, but many are literal descriptions. All of them share the characteristics of being compounds, and they most frequently occupy an entire half line of verse. They form by far the greater part of the "building-block" material of Old English poetry.

One can scan the glossary of Klaeber's third edition of *Beowulf* and find the nature of the noun epithet amply illustrated. A good place to begin is under the letter *h* with the "hilde-" (battle) compounds. We find "hilde-bord" (battle shield), "hilde-cumbor" (battle banner), "hilde-mece" (battle sword), "hilde-ræs" (battle rush), and twenty others. The difference between these straightforward compounds and the kennings is made clear when one compares "hilde-mece" (battle sword) with a kenning for sword, "hilde-leoma" (battle light). All are formulaic in that they are repeated, in *Beowulf* and elsewhere, and many have their counterparts in similar metrical patterns under different alliterative heads. Battle was one of the richest sources of formulas in Old English poetry; a number of words besides "hilde" convey the idea: "beado," "gud," "wæl," and so on. For "hilde-mece" (sword) we have "beado-mece." For "hilde-rinc" (warrior) we have "beado-rinc," and so on. They do not necessarily mean exactly the same thing; usually there are distinctive nuances. They provide the variation that is essential to a poetic based upon repetition.[4] Most of the equivalent epithets, as one would expect, reflect the concerns of a warrior culture: the attributes of the warrior and his weapons and the nature of his lord and his companions.

In *Beowulf* each person or important thing has its characteristic epithets, as in the Homeric poems, but with considerably more variety of choice for the poet.[5] The proper names are themselves epithets, like Beowulf (probably "beewolf," or bear), Hrothgar (glory spear), Unferth (mar peace). Beowulf's most common epithet is "bearn Ecgdeowes" (son of Ecgetheow), but with different alliteration and meter— and a different function for the hero—he is also "lidmanna helm" (protector of the seamen, line 1623) when he leads his men ashore in Denmark. Hrothgar is variously "Helm Scyldinga" (protector of the Scyldings, line 371), "wine Scyldinga" (friend of the Scyldings, line 30), "maga Healfdenes" (kinsman of Half-Dane, line 189), and "Deniga frean" (Lord of the Danes, line 271). Grendel is the "grimma gæst" (grim guest, line 102) and the "mære mearcstapa" (mighty wanderer of the wastes, line 103). Heorot, the famous hall built by Hrothgar, is "beahsele beorhta" (bright ring hall, i.e., hall where treasure is dispensed, line 1177). And so the list goes.

The Anglo-Saxon poet was thus capable of considerable variation and precision in his epithets for things and people. An unanswered question concerns the extent to which he may have indulged in irony in this respect, for certainly he was elsewhere fond of irony. The use of such an ordinary epithet as "helm Scyldinga" (protector of the Scyldings) for Hrothgar in line 1321, when Hrothgar is weeping and pouring out his troubles to Beowulf after Grendel's mother has killed Æschere (and there are examples of such seeming inappropriateness elsewhere) certainly appears to the modern eye as ironic. But we must be cautious in assigning modern intention and reaction to a poet who was telling his story twelve hundred years ago.

Adjectival epithets are frequently found in alliterative pairs in *Beowulf,* filling the half-line unit, as do their noun counterparts. Grendel is "grim ond grædig" (grim and greedy, line 121), and this family trait is observed also in his mother in the second episode, where she is "gifre ond galgmod" (greedy and gallows-minded, line 1277) as well. Heorot is "heah ond horngeap" (high and horn-gabled, line 82) and "geatolic ond goldfah" (splendid and gold-adorned, line 308). The dragon is "hat ond hreohmod" (hot and fierce in spirit, line 2296). Formulaic adjectives are otherwise normally paired alliteratively with nouns, as in "sigoreadig secg" (victorious warrior, line 1311), creating the half-line unit.

The adverbial formula is found in both phrase and clause forms. A common phrase pattern is the half-line time formula, e.g., "in geardagum" (in days of yore, line 1) and "lange hwile" (for a long while, line 16), likewise the general-place formula, "under wolcnum" (under the heavens, line 8), "ofer hronrade" (beyond the whale road or sea, line 10), and "geond þisne middangeard" (throughout this world, line 75). Phrases of purpose, or truncated clauses, are frequently half-line formulas as well: "folce to frofre" (as an aid to the people, line 14). Very occasionally an adverbial formula may occupy a whole line, as in line 197: "on þæm dæge þysses lifes" (in that time of this life). Adverbial clauses of purpose and result are also found among half-line formulas, e.g., "þæt ic þe sohte" (that I should seek you, line 417). A common formula of time is "syd þan morgen (aefen) cwom" (after morning or evening came), and there are many others.

The Sentence Formula

The sentence formula, both simple and complex, is obviously of great importance in the word hoard of the scop. Such sentences provide the necessary summaries and transitions and are the backbone of formulaic rhetoric. Many of them are short, half-line formulas. The best-known type is of the "þæt wæs god cyning" (that was a good king, line 11) sort; others are "ic þæt eall gemon" (I recall all that, line 2427) and "swa sceal mon don" (so shall man do, line 1172). Sentence formulas provide the usual means by which the poet expresses a variety of things. One person speaks to another in an almost invariable pattern: "Hrod gar maþelode, helm Scyldinga" (Hrothgar spoke, protector of the Scyldings, line 371); the passage of life is expressed in a sentence like "weox under wolcnum" (he waxed under the heavens, line 8); physical progression is normally a sentence formula, e. g., "wod under wolcnum" (he moved beneath the skies, line 714). The effect of weapons is usually expressed in short formulas, e.g., "Hra wide sprong" (The corpse rebounded far, line 1588).

In addition to the sentence formulas that are repeated verbatim or nearly so, there are many sentence patterns that serve the poet as outlines to be filled in, as it were, and that are used frequently enough to be considered formulaic. A negative, contrasting pattern beginning "not at all" or "not only" and containing "but," "after," "until," or "then" clauses is often employed in the ironic understatement that is so characteristic of the Anglo-Saxon poetic mode. Of Hilde-burh in the Finn episode we read (lines 1076-79a, italics ours):

> *Nalles* holinga Hoces dohtor
> meotodsceaft bemearn, sypðan morgen com,
> ða heo under swegle geseon meahte
> morþorbealo maga,

(*Not at all* without cause did the daughter of Hoc bemoan the decree of Fate *after* morning came, when she might see under heaven the slaughter of kinsmen.)

Describing the cowardly thanes who deserted Beowulf in his fight against the dragon, the poet tells us (lines 2596-98, italics ours):

> *Nealles* him on heape handgesteallan
> æðelinga bearn ymbe gestodon
> hildecystum, *ac* hy on holt bugon,

(*Not at all* did his comrades in arms, the children of warriors, stand about him [Beowulf] in martial glory, *but* they fled into the forest,)

Another common transitional pattern is "It was not long . . . until . . . ," describing ironically an immediate result (lines 2591b-92):

>   *Næs* ða long to ðon,
> *þæt* ða aglæcean hy eft gemetton.

(It was not long thence that the deadly fighters came together again.)

The clauses of the "when . . . then" and "since" and "until . . . that" patterns are frequently transitional in function and serve the poet as a means of encapsulating a brief bit of history that has a bearing on the immediate concern or of anticipating action to follow within the poem (or subsequent history outside the poem). The clauses allow rapid and rhetorically effective juxtaposition and bear much of the burden of the paralleling and contrasting technique that is a hallmark of the Anglo-Saxon style. An example of the first sort of use is seen in the introduction of Grendel (lines 102-108, italics ours):

> wæs se grimma gæst   Grendel haten,
> mære mearcstapa,   se þe moras heold,
> fen ond fæsten;   fifelcynnes eard
> wonsæli wer   weardode hwile,
> *siþðan* him Scyppend   forscrifen hæfde
> in Caines cynne—   þone cwealm gewræc
> ece Drihten,   þæs þe he Abel slog;

(The grim guest was called Grendel, the mighty stepper of the marches, who held the moors, the fens, and the fastnesses; the hapless one dwelt a while in the home of the monster race, *since* the Creator had cursed him, in the race of Cain— he avenged that murder, the eternal Lord, whereby Cain slew Abel;)

The "siþðan" (since) clause gives us the origin of Grendel and the reason that he bore the wrath of God, to which the poet refers later. A similar construction is subsequently used in describing the mother of Grendel (lines 1261-63).

The "oþ þæt" (until . . . that) clause has a similar function in that it allows for a brief summary but, of course, looks ahead. Of Beowulf's reign over the Geats, we learn (lines 2208-10, italics ours):

> he geheold tela
> fiftig wintra —wæs d'a frod cyning,
> eald eþelweard—, od' d'æt an ongan
> deorcum nihtum draca rics[i]an,

(he ruled well for fifty winters—he was a wise king, the old guardian of his people—*until* in the dark nights a dragon began to rule,)

The double function of summary and contrast—here powerful in its stark simplicity—could not be better illustrated.

Larger Rhetorical Patterns

The kinds of larger rhetorical structures that can be built from individual formulas and sentence patterns can be seen in the opening lines of *Beowulf.* To see how these structures are indeed formulaic, it will be necessary to look at introductions to other Old English poems as well.

Beowulf (lines 1-11, italics ours):

> *Hwæt,* we Gar-Dena *in geardagum,*
> þeodcyninga *þrym gefrunon,*
> *hu d'a æþelingas ellen fremedon!*
>   Oft Scyld Scefing sceaþena þreatum,
> monegum mægþum meodosetla ofteah,
> egsode eorl[as], *syd'd'an ærest weard'*
> feasceaft funden; he þæs frofre gebad,
> *weox under wolcnum* weord'myndum þah,
> od' þæt him æghwylc ymbsittendra
> ofer hronrade hyran scolde,
> gomban gyldan; þæt wæs god cyning!

(*Hark, we have learned of the glory* of the princes of the Spear-Danes *in days of yore, how the chiefs wrought mighty deeds.* Oft Scyld Scefing took the mead seats from troops of enemies, from many peoples; he terrified the earls, *after he first was found helpless*—he survived to be recompensed for that—*he grew under the heavens,* enjoyed high honor, *until* each of his neighbors over the whale road should obey him and pay tribute; that was a good king!)

The *Fates of the Apostles* (lines 1-8, italics ours):

> Hwæt! Ic þysne sang *sidgeomor fand*
> on seocum sefan, *samnode wide*
> *hu þa ædelingas ellen cyddon,*
> torhte ond tireadige. Twelfe wæron
> dædum domfæste, dryhtne gecorene,
> *leofe on life. Lof wide sprang,*
> miht ond mærdo, *ofer middangeard,*
> *þeodnes þegna,* þrym unlytel.[6]

(*Lo!* I this song, *weary of wandering* and sick in spirit, *made and put together from far and wide, of how the heroes,* bright and glorious, *made their courage known.* They were twelve in number, famed in deeds, chosen by the Lord, *beloved in life. Praise sprang wide,* the might and the fame, *throughout the world, of the Prince's thanes*—no small glory.)

Andreas (lines 1-6, italics ours):

> Hwæt! *we gefrunan on fyrndagum*
> *twelfe under tunglum* tireadige hæled,
> *þeodnes þegnas.* No hira þrym alæg

camprædenne ponne cumbol hneotan,
syd'd'an hie gedældon, swa him dryhten sylf,
heofona heahcyning, hlyt getæhte.[7]

(Lo! *We have heard, in days gone by, of the twelve under the stars,* glorious heroes, *the Lord's thanes.* Their glory did not fail in the field of battle when the banners clashed *after they had parted* as the Lord himself, the High King of Heaven, had commanded them.)

The Dream of the Rood (lines 1-3, italics ours):

Hwæt! Ic swefna cyst secgan wylle,
hwæt me gemætte to midre nihte,
syd'pan reordberend reste wunedon![8]

(Listen! I wish to tell the best of dreams *that came to me* in the middle of the night, *after the bearers of speech* [*men*] had gone to their rest.)

These poems have essentially little of theme and subject in common. *Beowulf* is the story of a warrior, *Andreas* and *Fates* are principally religious chronicles, and *Dream* is an almost mystical vision. Also, these passages have more differences in phrasing between them than close similarities. But the rhetorical structures are the same, and, as the italicized phrases show, the key formulas are essentially the same.

First, we cannot escape the opening "Hwæt!" Then, in *Beowulf* and *Andreas* follows the days-of-yore formula, "in geardagum," and "on fyrndagum." The source formula "we have learned" ("prym gefrunon" in *Beowulf* and "we gefrunan" in *Andreas*) is paralleled by variant formulas in the other two, "Ic pysne sang sid'geomor fand" ("Weary with the journey I made this song") in the *Fates of the Apostles* and "hwæt me gemætte" ("lo, I dreamed") in *The Dream of the Rood.* *Beowulf* and the *Fates* share an identical formula about what is learned—"hu ða æpelingas" (how the princes [performed]) in the same position, line 3a. Likewise, *Beowulf*'s "ellen fremedon" (performed deeds of valor) is paralleled by the *Fates* '"ellen cyðdon" (showed their courage), in line 3b—again, the same position. Next we consider the location formula "on earth" or "under heaven." In *Beowulf* it is "weox under wolcnum" (grew under the skies), and in *Andreas* we find "twelfe under tunglum" (twelve under the stars); in *Fates* it is "ofer middangeard" (throughout the middle yard). And, finally, the "since . . . (happened)" formula, which is rendered in *Beowulf* as "syððan ærest weard"(since he first was [found]), is rendered in *Andreas* as "syððan hie gedældon" (since they parted), and in *Dream* as "syðpan reordberend . . . reste wunedon" (after the speech-bearers had gone to rest).

In addition to the phrases in italics that are repeated or paralleled in one or another of the quoted passages, practically every phrase in each of the passages can be matched by a similar formula in several other Old English poems. Our purpose here, however, is to observe not only the verbal similarities but—equally important for illustrating the formulaic tradition of composition—the structural formula for opening a poem. It goes something like this: "Behold, . . . We [or I] have heard . . . in days of yore . . . how princes [or others] performed . . . deeds of glory . . . under the heavens . . . , since [or after] . . . [whatever happened at the beginning of the story or the circumstances of the telling]." This rhetorical pattern can be expanded or contracted as the poet wishes, and formulas selected and woven into the pattern. Although the passages quoted are introductory, the pattern can also be used for summary or transition within a narrative, as can been seen in lines 1769-81, 2384-90, and elsewhere in *Beowulf.*

Elaboration of Themes

In addition to such rhetorical structures, Old English poetry abounded in thematic formulas for everything of consequence in Anglo-Saxon life or story. By "thematic" we mean a nongrammatical contextual relationship of certain kennings, epithets, and symbolic objects. The poet was provided with ready-made formulas to elaborate the battle and its aftermath, sea-journeys, treasure-giving, the joy of the hall, funerals, introductions and farewells, etc. In describing a battle, for instance, the Anglo-Saxon poet would almost inevitably employ at some point the theme of the "beasts of battle."[9] These beasts are the animals that feed upon the bodies of the slain—the wolf, the raven, and the eagle. One of the most famous instances of the theme is found at the end of *The Battle of Brunanburh* (lines 60-65):

> Letan him behindan   hræw bryttian
> saluwigpadan,   þone sweartan hræfn,
> hyrnednebban,   and þane hasewanþadan,
> earn æftan hwit   æses brucan,
> grædigne guð'hafoc   and þæt græge deor,
> wulf on wealde.[10]

(They left behind them, to devour the corpses, the dark-coated, swart raven, horn-beaked, and the gray-coated, white-tailed eagle to enjoy the carrion, the greedy war hawk, and that gray beast, the wolf in the forest.)

This passage, with the three beasts of battle—the raven, the eagle, and the wolf—prepares the conclusion of the poem, for the poet is turning from the field. Like all other such formulas, it is amenable to variation of form and function as the poem demands. Probably because there are no fully described pitched battles between men in *Beowulf,* this theme is little used there, but the one full use of the formula is doubly impressive, for it does not describe a present field but is symbolic of the future fall of the Geatish nation, appearing near the end of the poem where the poet prophesies, through the voice of the messenger who announces Beowulf's fall and the dragon's demise, the coming doom of the Geats (lines 3021b-3027):

> Forðon sceall gar wesan
> monig morgenceald   mundum bewunden,
> hæfen on handa,   nalles hearpan sweg,
> wigend weccean,   ac se wonna hrefn
> fus ofer faegum   fela reordian,
> earne secgan,   hu him æt æte speow,
> þenden he wið wulf   wæl reafode.

(Therefore, many a spear, cold in the morning, shall be wound about with fingers, raised in hands; not at all shall the sound of the harp stir the warriors, but instead the dark raven, eager above the fated, shall speak much, shall say to the eagle how it sped him at the feasting when he and the wolf plundered the slaughtered.)

The theme, though rooted in a context of battle description, is clearly more variable in its usefulness than to be merely descriptive; in *Beowulf* the ancient theme has become symbolic in its function as in its nature. For ironic contrast it is joined with the theme of the joys of the hall, whose symbol is the harp. The gladsome sound of the harp is gone, and in its place is the snarling of the animals of the battlefield. Grammatically the passage is constructed on the "nalles . . . ac" (not at all this . . . but that) formulaic pattern. These are only two examples of formulaic themes that abound in

Beowulf (the "joys of the hall" theme itself appears on several occasions, as in lines 89-98, 491-98, 642-45, 1980-83, and 2262-63, etc.). The sea-voyage themes are twice elaborately done and well illustrate the variety available to the scop within a thematic pattern. Although certain formulas are repeated, and although the structure of the passages is identical, most of the words are different. The structure is simply this: the boat was in the water; the men loaded it and steered it into the sea; there it was urged by the wind, until the time came that the seamen could see the cliffs of the shore. Each of the steps in the pattern is expressed in a formula, and the pattern itself is constructed around an "until . . . that" clause. The similar formulas are italicized. First, Beowulf's journey to Denmark (lines 210-28, italics ours):

Fyrst forð gewat;	*flota wæs on yðum,*
bat under beorge.	Beornas gearwe
on stefn stigon, —	streamas wundon,
sund wið sande;	secgas bæron
on bearm nacan	beorhte frætwe,
guðsearo geatolic;	guman ut scufon,
weras on wilsið	wudu bundenne.
Gewat þa ofer wægholm	winde gefysed
flota famiheals	fugle gelicost,
oð þæt ymb antid	oþres dogores
wundenstefna	gewaden hæfde,
þæt ða liðende	land gesawon,
brimclifu blican,	beorgas steape,
side sænæssas;	þa wæs sund liden,
eoletes æt ende.	Þanon up hraðe
Wedera leode	on wang stigon,
sæwudu sældon, —	syrcan hrysedon,
guðgewædo;	Gode þancedon
þaes þe him yþlade	eaðe wurdon.

150

(Time passed; *the ship was on the waves,* the boat under the cliff. The warriors eagerly stepped aboard; the currents wound, the sea against the sand; the men bore into the bosom of the ship bright ornaments, splendid battle armor; the warriors on their sought-for journey pushed off the well-made ship. The *foamy-necked floater* departed over the waves, most like a bird, urged on by the wind, *until* in due time on the next day *the ship with the curved prow* had progressed *so that the voyagers* saw the land, the shining sea cliffs, the steep hills, the wide headlands; then was the sea crossed, the travel at an end. Thence the men of the Weders quickly stepped on the land and tied up the ship. Their armor, the weeds of war, rattled; they gave thanks to God that the crossing had been an easy one for them.)

This is surely one of the better-known passages in *Beowulf.* The references made to it often imply that it is full of the rhetoric of sea travel, but actually the description of crossing is confined to lines 216-21: "The foamy-necked floater departed over the waves, most like a bird, urged on by the wind." We are clearly deluded by the famous "foamy-necked floater." Aside from this kenning the only other figure is a rather rare example of an Old English simile, "fugle gelicost" (most like a bird). We turn from this passage with its emphasis on preparation and battle spirit to the second sea voyage, which takes Beowulf and his men home after they have rid Hrothgar's land of monsters (lines 1896-1913, italics ours):

> *Pa wæs on sande   sægeap naca*
> hladen herewædum   *hringedstefna,*
> mearum ond madmum;   mæst hlifade
> ofer Hrodgares   hordgestreonum.
> He þæm batwearde   bunden golde
> swurd gesealde,   þæt he sydþan wæs

on meodubence   maþme þy weorþra,
yrfelafe.   Gewat him on naca
drefan deop wæter,   Dena land ofgeaf.
Þa wæs be mæste   merehrægla sum,
segl sale fæst;   sundwudu þunede;
no þær wegflotan   wind ofer yðum
sides getwæfde;   sægenga for,
fleat famigheals   forð ofer yðe,
bundenstefna   ofer brimstreamas,
þæt hie Geata clifu   ongitan meahton,
cuþe næssas;   ceol up geþrang
lyftgeswenced,   on lande stod.

(*Then the roomy ship* loaded with war weeds *was on the sands —
the ring-prowed vessel* loaded with horses and treasure; the mast
stood high above Hrothgar's precious hoard goods. He [Beowulf]
gave to the boat ward a sword wound with gold so that afterward
at the mead bench the guardian was held more worthy because of
this treasure, the heirloom. He boarded the ship, to drive through
the deep water, he departed the land of the Danes. Then the sea
garment, a sail bound with a rope, was at the mast. The sea wood
resounded; the wind over the waves did not force the wave floater
from its course; the sea traveler went on, the *foamy-necked one*
floated onward over the waves, *the well-joined prow* over the
sea streams, *until they might see the Geatish cliffs,* the known
headlands. The keel, urged by the wind, pressed upward and
stood on the land.)

We have a repetition of the "foamy-necked" figure, but the
other terms are varied; the ship is "ring-prowed" or "curved-
prowed," the ship is "sundwudu," the "wave-floater," and so
on. The return voyage is described with considerably more
detail than is the voyage in the preceding passage; in addition
to describing the loading of the vessel and its arrival "on
lande," the poet gives six lines of carefully varied description

to the ship, the wind, and the sea. We learn that the ship has a sail, a "sea garment," and we hear the sound of the ship straining against the sea ("sundwudu punede," the sea wood groaned, or resounded). The only sound in the first passage is the grim noise of the rattling of armor. The effect of this is not hard to find: in the first passage all attention is to the coming struggle; here the spirit is one of release.

In addition to elaborate thematic set pieces such as these, scattered throughout *Beowulf* one finds many short tropes, frequently of a moralizing nature. These are often in the form of sentences, such as, "Swa sceal mon don," (So shall a man do, line 1172), or, "Swa he nu git ded" (So He [God] still does, line 1058), in passages illustrating proper conduct in a situation or summarizing the actions of God or the course of fate, over which man has no control. Such gnomic themes are "the uselessness of buried gold" (lines 3058-60, 2275-77, 3167-68), "the dangers of disturbing dragons" (lines 2836-42, 3050-60), and the "unfæge eorl" (the undoomed warrior who may escape fate if his courage avails him, lines 2291-93, 572-73).[11]

Although the various stories intruded into *Beowulf,* such as the Finn episode, the story of Offa, or the story of Hama, have no place in the present discussion, having been considered in our treatment of the background of the poem, in a sense these "digressions" are much like the moral tropes in that they illustrate good and bad behavior, wise and foolish conduct. They are elaborate analogies that, while not exactly formulaic in nature, serve the purposes of shorter formulaic themes. There are other formulaic aspects of *Beowulf,* but these seem to us to be of most significance for the modern reader.

Having surveyed some of the materials of Old English poetry, let us now see how these materials are used in *Beowulf* and what kind of poetry they produce. In the preceding chapter we have seen something of how Old English verse works; its structure is that of balanced building blocks of complementary meter united by alliteration. The smaller formulaic units, as we have seen, form many of these building blocks, each usually occupying a half line. As anyone familiar with the medieval ballad (or modern ballads, for that matter) knows, much of the ballad is of preformed phrases and whole lines that do not themselves move the poem. These formulas provide a brief stasis in the progression of the narrative and cause the "hitching" effect that is so noticeable in ballads. In *Beowulf* the formula likewise provides the reflection more often than the action, though, as we have seen, Old English poems use a number of formulaic sentences to get the action under way.

Normally the *Beowulf* poet balances an epithet half line with a verb phrase half line, as in lines 2397-2400:

> Swa he nid'a gehwane   genesen hæfde
> slid'ra geslyhta,   sunu Ecgd'iowes
> ellenweorca,   od' d'one anne dæg
> þe he wid' þam wyrme   gewegan sceolde.

(So he each of battles had survived, each terrible conflict, the son of Ecgtheow, each courageous work, until one day that he should meet with the dragon.)

The "he" in line 2397a is balanced by its epithet "sunu Ecgd'iowes" in line 2398b. In this brief passage there are two formulas roughly comparable in meaning to "nid'a gehwane": "slid'dra geslyhta" and "ellenweorca," both in the a verses. All the b verses except for lines 2398b are occupied by the verb or adverbial phrases. The verses cannot be read rapidly, for the formulas give a parenthetical effect in their reinforcing role. The movement of the verse is therefore largely incremental.

154

As we consider the method of the *Beowulf* poet, we realize that the paralleling characteristics of the formula are shared by the other rhetorical elements. We have observed that the themes introduced as ornament parallel or contrast the character or action that they comment upon. An example is the poet's use of the theme of the joys of the harp in the hall as ironic contrast in lines 89-98; it is the very joy of the men and the noise of the harp that brings their catastrophe, for it arouses Grendel. The larger episodes function in much the same way, as the Finn episode comments on Hrothgar's court, and the Sigemund story anticipates Beowulf and the dragon. It is not even beyond the bounds of possibility that, as Tolkien suggested, the two parts of Beowulf, paralleling one another, reflect this fundamental quality of Old English poetry.[12]

It might well seem, from our discussion, that the kind of poetry that the Germanic tradition produced would inevitably be slow, tedious, and dully repetitive. It has, indeed, been argued that *Beowulf* is validly appreciated only as barbaric poetry, possessing merely an unsophisticated irony.[13] Old English poetry was very far from being wholly formulaic, however, and the *Beowulf* poet in particular possessed great resources of poetic vocabulary for variation. He was also capable of dispensing with the elaborate parallel movement of his verse to rush headlong into the action, as in lines 1441-42:

> Gyrede hine Beowulf
> eorlgewædum,   nalles for ealdre mearn

(Beowulf then dressed himself in earl's weeds—not at all did he care for his life.)

Here the formula "nalles for ealdre mearn" does not interrupt Beowulf's quick arming for the fray but for emphasis is left to line 1442b.

It cannot be denied, however, that the poetry of *Beowulf* is quite different from the post-Renaissance English verse to which we are accustomed. The formulaic nature of the Old English language results in a certain lack of that precision which we have come to expect from the poetic imagination. The very nature of compound words seems to involve a semantic compromise. The effect of *Beowulf*, like that of other Old English poems, results from a building of meaning rather than an assertion of it. The poet swings between ironic understatement and hyperbole. He tends frequently to tell us what things are not and what people did not do, leaving us to supply the positive.

Although it must be admitted that Old English kennings and epithets frequently clog up the movement of the narrative, in *Beowulf* particularly the modifiers tend to be cumulative, each adding a quality or aspect to character or action. This incremental effect is seen in a long passage already cited, that of Beowulf's sea voyage to Hrothgar's court. The poet uses in the passage a variety of kennings for the boat: It is "flota" at line 210, "bat" at line 211, "nacan" (of the ship) at line 214, "wudu bundenne" at line 216, "flota famiheals" at line 218, and "wundenstefna" at line 220. Now "flota," "bat," and "nacan" do not much improve on one another, for they all rather nakedly mean "boat" or "ship." But the poet is at the beginning simply saying that the boat is there, on the waves in shallow water, being loaded. When the boat begins to move, the poet selects kennings that focus attention on the ship itself, its ornament and motion. The poet's imagination has been awakened. The ship is a craftsman's work, we learn, "wudu bundenne," well-joined wood. As it moves into the open sea, the "famiheals" or "foamy-necked" image pictures for us the waves being sliced by the long prow of the ship. This prow is itself the next image, the curved stem of "wundenstefna." All the words are kennings for "ship," but they tell us, in themselves, something of what is happening. They reflect the changing focus of the narrative. We could arrange these figures in their order, remove them from their context, and learn that the "flota" has become "foamy-necked," that the well-built ship of "wudu bundenne" is now represented by another aspect, its curved prow—the "wundenstefna," suggestive of the outward thrust of the ship. When at the end of the journey the ship is tied to the Danish shore, it becomes "saewudu" or "sea wood," simply another kenning for "ship" but one that now has the nuance "seaworthy wood," wood that has been tried. The incremental effect of the series of images suggests the progress of the narrative.

In a similar way the repetitive aspect of sentences and larger patterns can be cumulative and extremely effective. The first-time reader of *Beowulf* is impressed by the twice-repeated formula of movement when Grendel's approach to the high-gabled hall of Hrothgar is being described in lines 702-21a: "Com on wanre niht / scriðan sceadugenga" (There came in the dim night stealthily moving the shadow goer); "Þa com of more / under misthleopum / Grendel gongan" (Then came from the moor under the dark mists, Grendel moving); and, finally, "Com þa to recede / rinc siðian / dreamum bedæled" (There came then to the hall that warrior bereft of joy). The effect of the repeated patterns is undeniably powerful, and it is a typical, though spectacular, example of the *Beowulf* poet's method.[14]

The result of incremental aspect of the poetic method is that the individual epithet or phrase has more emphasis—more time in the reader's or hearer's consciousness. The reader or hearer, in short, is required to play a rather active role in the poem, almost a creative one. The tradition of oral poetry depends on an alert, participating, cooperating hearer. To a greater extent than with poetry whose tradition is totally literary, poetry that has its origins—in however dim a past— in the give-and-take between performer and audience depends for the completion of its meaning upon its audience. Therefore, particularly for early Germanic poetry, the best possible preparation that the student can make is to acquaint himself with as many of the surviving poems as possible, either in the original or in modern versions. He can then share with the poet a knowledge of the legends, recognize the context of kennings, and appreciate the unexpected variation.

CHAPTER 10

Interpretations and Criticism
of *Beowulf* in Our Own Time

IT would be satisfying to begin a survey of modern *Beo-wulf* criticism without saying the obvious, which is that contemporary approaches to the poem owe much to the shape of *Beowulf* criticism set over forty years ago in a single paper, J. R. R. Tolkien's *"Beowulf:* The Monsters and the Critics" (1936), but it would be misleading to do so. Although the historical scholarship—German, French, English, and American—of the late nineteenth and early twentieth centuries shows much perceptive, purely literary insight, it is not an exaggeration to say that before Tolkien's Sir Israel Gollancz Memorial lecture there existed no more than a dozen important considerations of the poem purely or largely as a literary work. Since Tolkien there have been no more than a dozen important additions to the earlier historical or folkloristic studies. Although it may have nothing to do with the foregoing observations, it is striking that the German voices so preponderant in earlier *Beowulf* scholarship have in later years become almost still, an exception being A. Pirkhofer's analysis of character portrayal (see the Select Bibliography for works referred to in this chapter).

At any rate, Tolkien's essay, emphasizing the reasonableness of the poet's materials in relation to the themes of the poem, the balance of the parts and the unity of effect and assuming a single poem by a single author, caught a critical tide at the full. The 1930s were, of course, a very active period of literary criticism—the golden period of those critics who to a great extent formed our ways of looking at literature—T. S. Eliot, Ezra Pound, John Crowe Ransom, Cleanth Brooks—in short, the founders of the New Criticism—who were then approaching the zenith of their influence. *Beowulf,* hitherto protected by the barriers of language from much "belletristic" criticism, became more accessible through Tolkien's brilliant demonstration that it was, above all other things, a poem. Because it was still in Old English, there was no great rush by the major new critics to consider it, but the way was prepared for those whose interest lay mainly in the critical analysis of poetry. The careful studies of style and structure by Joan Blomfield and C. C. Batchelor were doubtless already in preparation before Tolkien delivered his paper, and A. E. DuBois's fine study of the unity of the poem had appeared in 1934. But there is a sense in which all criticism since Tolkien's has either affirmed or attacked his views.

Our present concern is with the development of primarily literary criticism—thematic and technical—of the twentieth century, and chiefly with the various movements of the past thirty years. It seems to us that there are three headings under which *Beowulf* criticism of this period can be placed with a minimum of Procrustean fitting. One is that of general studies of style, diction, theme, and form. The second is the literary role of Christian themes in the poem, and the third is the application to *Beowulf* of the theories of the "oral-formulaic" school (already discussed in chapter 9). These categories obviously overlap to some degree, and our discussion by no means attempts a comprehensive survey but selects illustrative treatments.

Beowulf *as "Literature"*

The acceptance of Tolkien's assumptions about the nature of *Beowulf*—that it is the work of a conscious artist, that it shows certain principles of unity and balance together with one or more important themes, and that it strives for a particular effect—has not been total by any means. Two essays of the 1950s, those of T. M. Gang ("Approaches to *Beowulf*") and J. C. van Meurs ("*Beowulf* and Literary Criticism"), essentially challenged the application of any kind of purely literary criticism to *Beowulf* or to Old English poetry. More recently, in a short, acerbic book *(The Structure of Beowulf)*, a great Anglo-Saxon scholar, Kenneth Sisam, delivered a sometimes brilliant and sometimes only perverse attack on thirty years of literary analysis of the poem. In general, however, the trend of criticism has been steadily that of close analysis and interpretation of *Beowulf* as a poem. This criticism has been frequently profitable in its insights, but occasionally it has deserved Sisam's strictures.

Two books on *Beowulf*—Arthur G. Brodeur's *The Art of Beowulf* (1959) and Edward B. Irving's *A Reading of Beowulf* (1968)—have shown what can be achieved by imaginative but sober study of the language and structure of the poem. Perhaps the best book ever written on early English poetry is Brodeur's. It deals illuminatingly with the language of the poet, emphasizing his originality in spite of, and sometimes because of, the traditional materials and formulas of the Germanic poet. Brodeur appends to his book a valuable checklist of compounds and epithets that support his claims about the *Beowulf* poet's capacity for variation and "originality" of diction. Brodeur finds a unity of theme and structure not unlike that proposed by Tolkien and comes down solidly on the side of those who argue that the poet was a single, inspired man, that he was a Christian of the eighth-century variety but not an allegorist. The poet, in Brodeur's view, was a lettered man, not the illiterate singer favored by the proponents of the "oral-formulaic" theory. Brodeur argues that the poet carefully related the episodes and digressions to the main narrative and the thematic material. Although he does not deal with theological surmise, Brodeur finds the Christian implications of the poem obvious. He is content to describe the poem's theme thus:

> I think, with Tolkien, that the poet meant that this [Beowulf's futile but heroic struggle] is life's way with men. The most heroic life must close in death, as Beowulf reminded Hrothgar; he who is permitted to "achieve some share of renown before death," and to face his last hour with fortitude, conquers, though he perishes. And however nobly man may strive toward noble ends, unless those be God's ends, man strives in vain. But it is the courage to strive, not success, which marks and ennobles the hero.[1]

Brodeur's contribution lies in his discussion of the parts of the poem, the poet's artistry in diction, in contrast, in weaving together the elements of allusion and anticipation in individual passages. Most of criticism since Brodeur has revealed awareness of his work.

A book somewhat like Brodeur's in its analysis of the poem is Irving's *A Reading of Beowulf.* Irving attempts to discover the essence of the poet's art by study of typical stylistic devices and their relation to the themes of the poem. For instance, the rhetorical pattern of "until" clauses represents the poet's use of sentence structure to emphasize oppositions, whereas patterns of redundance emphasize continuity. Irving argues that the balance of the line and the formulaic devices seem always to aim at definition, achieved seldom by a direct statement but usually through either cumulative effect or the statement of alternatives and oppositions. This essentially *reinforcing,* allusive style of the poet is the main subject of Irving's book, and Irving's analysis is usually convincing. His study serves as a useful introduction to the style of the *Beowulf* poet, though occasionally Irving's assumptions seem a trifle broad.

Many interesting shorter studies have appeared in the past thirty years. We can do no more than cite a few of the better and more influential ones, with a cautionary example of the embarrassing extremes to which close reading and thematic structural analysis have on occasion brought us. We could not avoid mentioning *en masse* the essays of Adrien Bonjour, who is nearly always genially provocative and instructive. The best examples of his thoughtful readings of the poem may be found in his collected papers *(Twelve Beowulf Papers)* and in his monograph *The Digressions in Beowulf.* Throughout his work Bonjour is committed to a sympathetic understanding of the poet and assumes that, whenever there occurs something that does not readily yield to the logical demands of the modern reader, a careful study will usually reveal the inconsistency or digression to be an acceptable development seen within the framework of the poet's themes, structure, and techniques. And one is more often than not convinced by Bonjour's skillful arguments, even, finally, within the demands that the twentieth-century reader makes upon narrative.

A very interesting concept of the structure of *Beowulf* is contained in R. M. Lumiansky's "The Dramatic Audience of *Beowulf,*" in which he argues that the suspense effect of the poem is obtained partly through the poet's inclusion of a "dramatic" audience for the three fights, in each instance an audience whose security depends upon the outcome of the fight. B. J. Timmer's "*Beowulf:* The Poem and Its Poet" treats the structure and the theme of the poem as essentially a compromise between the poem's pagan and Christian elements. Somewhat similarly, H. L. Rogers, in his "Beowulf's Three Great Fights," sees the form of the poem as a failure because of this compromise. Kemp Malone's *"Beowulf"* again treats the poem's theme and structure as a result of the attempt to compromise pagan Germanic and Christian heritage, glorifying each.

An essay with something of the same concerns is John Leyerle's "Beowulf the Hero and the King" which sees the theme of the poem as "the fatal contradiction at the core of the heroic society" in which the impelling code demands for the hero individual achievement and glory, whereas society demands a king who achieves for the common good.[2] Leyerle's "The Interlace Structure of *Beowulf*" sees in the verbal patterns of Old English poetry a parallel to the interlace pattern of ornamentation in the Celtic and Germanic art of the age of *Beowulf.* A more general analysis of the form of the poem is H. G. Wright's "Good and Evil; Light and Darkness; Joy and Sorrow in *Beowulf,*" which does not insist upon close interpretation but discusses the relationships of mood and tone in the poem with its structure, a structure that, Wright argues, though not casual, is nevertheless not tight and mechanical. The dominating moods of the poem tend to govern the organization by the poet, who

has no meticulous design, worked out with mathematical precision. . . . The three groups of opposites that have been examined are seen to intersect but not to coincide; and though they contribute to a fundamental unity, as the poem advances, with the deepening of the elegiac strain sorrow gets the upper hand. . . . One last survivor after the other passes in sombre procession, and Fate hangs more and more heavily over all mankind. The word *geomor* [sad] and its derivatives echo at intervals like a mournful bell, and the whole culminates in the dirge for the fall of a great king.[3]

On many occasions the twentieth-century appreciation of complexity and subtlety in literature has led to a reading of *Beowulf* that has amounted to the creation of a new poem with little resemblance to the eighth-century masterpiece left to us. Chiefly this outcome has stemmed from a refusal to accept the characters of the poem as the author has created them—fine, solid characters, no doubt, but not very complex or much given to musings and ulterior motives. An instance of this sort of interpretation is James O. Rosier's "Design for Treachery: The Unferth Intrigue."[4] Rosier's thesis is that the fight with Grendel's mother is given added complexity by the treachery of Unferth, who, humiliated by Beowulf's besting him in both boast and example, deliberately lends Beowulf his own sword, Hrunting, in full knowledge that it will fail and the hope that the failure will lead to Beowulf's death. This is the sort of double- and triple-layer treachery we could expect in a John Le Carré novel, but scarcely in *Beowulf.* To interpret Unferth's action in this way, the reader must extract both Unferth and Beowulf from the poem and ignore what the poet specifically says. We must forget that the poet tells us, in describing the sword, the famous Hrunting (lines 1458-61):

> þæt wæs an foran   ealdgestreona;
> ecg wæs iren,   atertanum fah,
> ahyrded heaposwate;   næfre hit æt hilde ne swac
> manna ængum   þara þe hit mid mundum bewand,

(that was among the first of ancient treasures; its edge was iron, decorated with poison [?] stripes, hardened by battle sweat [blood]; never had it failed in battle any of the men who wielded it with their hands,)

Quite apart from any lingering resentment that Unferth may have had, this is a gracious gesture.[5] Clearly the poet implies that if *any* sword will do the job then Hrunting is that sword. There is subtlety and art in the poet's treatment of Unferth's sword, but it is less devious than Rosier's argument claims. A minor theme of the poet is that Beowulf never has luck with swords—his battle strength is too great, they break beneath his swing. Another is that Grendel's kin cannot be killed by human weapons, not even by the greatest. And, of course, Unferth is not entirely selfless; it is possible that his motive, or part of it, is to share in the glory of Beowulf, even if vicariously. We see in the poem, in Beowulf's gift to the shore guard when he reembarks, what honor accrues to warriors at the bench who possess weapons that have achieved mighty deeds (lines 1900-1903a):

> He þæm batwearde   bunden golde
> swurd gesealde,   þæt he syd'pan wæs
> on meodubence   mapme þy weorpra,
> yrfelafe.

(He gave to the guardian of the boat a sword decorated with gold, so that he [the guardian] was ever after held in greater esteem at the mead bench because of this heirloom.)

Therefore, one does not have to assume that Unferth's quarrelsome nature and concern for his own glory have been suddenly transformed into something noble. But one does not have to assume either an elaborate scheme of irony that serves as reverse counterpoint to what the poet again and again expressly tells us.

But it is not in opposition to such excesses of critical subtlety that Kenneth Sisam argues in his short, truculent book *The Structure of Beowulf* (1965). Sisam would deny the basic assumptions under which most critics have worked for many years. He would deny that the poem has the care-

166

ful, conscious balance and unity that lie at the heart of the assumptions of most recent interpreters and also that the poem has a deliberately worked out theme. He attacks what is perhaps the weakest point in Tolkien's lecture, the argument that the two-part structure of the poem parallels in any way the divided line of its verse, though that is only a bit of speculation on Tolkien's part. He also denies Tolkien's view that the poem's central concern is "the battle, hopeless in this world, of man against evil" (Sisam's phrasing).[6] Sisam suggests that the critics' conclusion that the poem as it stands does not, frankly, measure up to the standards of poetry that the critics assume for their own time and that, therefore, the poem must be *read* so as to come up to those standards seems to be behind most recent literary criticism. Sisam argues that such modern standards are inappropriate and that the appreciation and taste of the Anglo-Saxons were quite different from ours. Further, Sisam shrewdly suggests what many have felt—that the pressure upon the scholar to publish in his field has brought about a corresponding pressure to *find* something new and that "one of its consequences is a tendency to speculation on the things that are not expressed in *Beowulf*."[7]

The Structure of Beowulf deals with other matters, but its attack on the subtlety of contemporary criticism is our present concern. For all his cogency and telling style, however, Sisam is too sweeping and extreme in his attack. He seems to dismiss much of the elaborate parallelism of the poet's digressions as just that—digressions—in the manner of a teacher of rhetoric. There are simply too many instances of foreshadowing and careful contrast for Sisam's destructive analysis to be ultimately convincing. Further, not all the appreciations of parallels and contrasts in the digressions of *Beowulf* are products of the new fever in *Beowulf* studies, as a glance at Klaeber's notes or Donald K. Fry's *Bibliography* (1969)

167

will show, so that it is not really a question, as Sisam would seem to have it, of a modern critic's miraculous discovery of subtlety and skill that had lain unappreciated during the 150 years of *Beowulf* criticism. Sisam tends to lower the artistry of the poem by too much, by whatever standards are used, and in his summation he states clearly that the structure of the poem is just not all that good; it is inferior, for instance, to that of the *Odyssey, Sir Gawain,* and the *Song of Roland.* One would grant the first but, we think, boggle at the other two; for comparison of *Beowulf* with *Gawain,* a deliberately conceived, single-theme poem if there ever was one, is not quite fair, and most students of medieval literature would give *Beowulf* at least equal marks with *Roland* in its welding two large actions and their attendant themes into a single work. The *Roland* poet's task, in fact, seems a good deal easier in a way, and the victory of Charlemagne and the distribution of justice, after the action at Roncevalles, seem a falling-off greater than Beowulf's fight with the dragon after the Heorot episodes.

Nonetheless, Sisam's book should be required reading of all students of *Beowulf,* along with those of Brodeur, Bonjour, and Irving. It is salutary to be reminded that Anglo-Saxon ideas of what constituted a good poem were not necessarily ours and that much of the subtlety discovered in *Beowulf* may be in the beholder's eye rather than in the poet's plan. Even when the creative artist achieves an effect, he may do so more by intuition than by the elaborate conscious artistry assumed by many modern critics. Overconscious art, in fact, is likely to be second or third rate.

Christianity as a Theme

Many of Sisam's animadversions are aimed at the current school of Christian exegesis of the poem and the interpretation of the poem as an exposition of ideal behavior, a manual for princes. In a brief essay he surveys the evidence in the text of *Beowulf* for a Christian intention by the poet and concludes that "in this work the poet was not much concerned with Christianity and paganism."[8] Most criticism of the twentieth century, in reaction to the "monkish interpolation" way of explaining the Old Testament allusions in *Beowulf,* which was most exhaustively asserted by F. A. Blackburn in "The Christian Coloring in the *Beowulf*", has assumed a certain Christian awareness by the *Beowulf* poet (as opposed to a redactor), if not a spirit of evangelism. The moderate position with respect to the poem's Christianity was best expressed by Marie P. Hamilton in "The Religious Principle in *Beowulf*." Earlier H. Munro Chadwick, in *The Heroic Age,* had supposed that the bulk of the poem had a prior, pagan existence and then was made over for a Christian audience by a Christian poet. Dorothy Whitelock, in *The Audience of Beowulf,* makes an impressive argument that the audience of *Beowulf* was thoroughly acquainted with Christian doctrines and defines the poet of *Beowulf* as "the Christian author who was responsible for giving the poem the general shape and tone in which it has survived."[9] Larry D. Benson, in ("The Pagan Coloring of *Beowulf*," in *Old English Poetry*) put the shoe on the other foot by suggesting that in fact much of the expressly pagan material in the poem was put there by the Christian poet to arouse sympathy for the heroic ideals of the past.

This growing acceptance of a close awareness of Christian doctrines in the poet and his audience seems to be linked with an assumption by the critics of a single work by a single poet, whatever preexisting materials the poet may have recast for his poem. This assumption, as we have seen, is also held by most other, not specifically Christian-oriented criticism of recent times. Further, critics have long noted a certain didactic tendency in the poem (one calls to mind such essays as L. L. Schücking's "Das Königsideal in *Beowulf*"), and, not unnaturally, the dominant interest of most modern scholars concerned with the nature of Beowulf's Christianity has been the poem's Christian *theme* as the unifying, overriding structural concern of the poet. Much of this writing has assumed, or argued, at least a partial allegorical direction in the poem. Among such studies can be mentioned Morton W. Bloomfield's "*Beowulf* and Christian Allegory: An Interpretation of Unferth," Maurice B. McNamee's "*Beowulf*—An Allegory of Salvation?" Lewis E. Nicholson's "The Literal Meaning and Symbolic Structure of *Beowulf*," and, especially, Margaret E. Goldsmith's essays, which have been gathered and expanded in her *The Mode and Meaning of Beowulf* (1970). Particularly in Nicholson's and Goldsmith's studies are the overt, later medieval allegorical structures assumed. We have already indicated what we think of such elaborate allegorical interpretations of *Beowulf*, Christian or otherwise, but we should perhaps pause here to consider the inherent weakness of such interpretation as applied to *Beowulf*.

Biblical exegesis was, of course, rife in the eighth century, though not nearly as pervasive as it became three or four centuries later. Christian allegory was very well established. There is little evidence, however, of such nonclassical secular materials as those of *Beowulf* being anywhere cast into a deliberately allegorical form. We cannot, of course, speak to the question of the reaction of the contemporary audience or reader to *Beowulf*, but what little evidence is provided by the manuscript in which our poem is found suggests that whoever made up the codex probably looked upon the poem as an exciting story (Benson suggests, in "The Pagan Coloring of *Beowulf*," that the poem's pagan qualities perhaps accounted for its preservation). In the second part of manuscript Vitellius A.15, *Beowulf* is the fourth item, preceded by the fragment on Saint Christopher, the dog-headed saint; *The Marvels of the East;* and the letter of Alexander to Aristotle, and followed by the *Judith* fragment. All the works in this part were copied by two scribes, who apparently divided their work around the middle of *Beowulf.* There is little in these materials that would seem to put the reader (or hearer) into a receptive frame of mind for doctrinal instruction, though, of course quite unexpected things can be used for such purposes. The emphasis seems to be on the marvelous, on the exciting story of the spectacular and dramatic. Allegorists have not ignored the questions of *Beowulf*'s fellows in the unique manuscript. Karl Brunner, in "Why Was *Beowulf* Preserved?" argued that *Beowulf* was preserved for its moral instruction, that the *Beowulf* codex was primarily devoted to Christian heroes. One can, of course, clearly make a case for Saint Christopher, and *Judith,* but *The Marvels of the East* and Alexander's letter require the most subtle of doctors to transform them into Christian doctrine. We are inclined to the opinion of Sisam, in *Studies in the History of Old English Literature,* that the Saint Christopher, *The Marvels of the East,* and Alexander's letter are associated by their common stories of dog-headed cannibals.[10] *Judith*'s association is less clear; although, as Sisam concedes, Holofernes was no monster, the beheading of a larger-than-life figure might well give scribes reason enough to include it after the story of Beowulf's fights with the trolls.

Goldsmith, of course, quotes Brunner with approval. But in any case, the evidence of the codex could hardly be regarded as conclusive. The allegorical interpretation stands or falls on the coherence and logic of its analysis of the poem itself. And the bulk of her analysis is usually, so to speak, the windup before the pitch, in which she draws together a vast collection of theological materials that the poet could conceivably have known or that might have contributed to the thinking of his age on doctrine and so have provided the basis for the poet's thought. About these materials it is difficult to speak; certainly they *might* have functioned in the way that Goldsmith claims that they did. And her discussion of Christian symbolism, supported by some forays into anthropology, is learned and interesting. In the last chapters of her book, however, particularly in "Structure and Meaning," she fails, in our opinion, to make her case. She claims not only moral but allegorical significance, and it is against the latter claim that the reader is likely to rebel. For Goldsmith in her argument that Beowulf, in spite of his superhuman physical powers, is at the end, as Hrothgar prophesied, alas, all too human and succumbs to the lure of worldly wealth and is therefore off his guard when approached by the slayer Death, comes into violent conflict with the specific language of the poet. In arguing that Beowulf is overmastered by his lust for the dragon's gold, she makes her curious case that Beowulf is the just man who ultimately proves unequal to his responsibility of kingship and who, though he will be pardoned by God, brings sorrow to a whole nation. This interpretation, bolstered by no matter how many quotations from the fathers and theologians and by the poet's own comments on the nature of wealth, seems to be contradicted by what the poet tells us about the actions of Beowulf.

First, of course, Beowulf does not go on a treasure hunt. His motives are clearly described by the poet as those that move him in the first half of the poem—the call of responsibility and the desire for glory, two of the three characteristics particularized in the last three lines of the poem as the poet simply and movingly records the tribute of Beowulf's people. Among these tributes is not that he was "the most desirous of wealth and power" but instead that he was "most considerate of his people," "gentlest and mildest of men," and "most eager for praise." Surely here if anywhere the

172

poet, if he had allegorical intentions, would have stated them clearly. Goldsmith's *significatio* is missing. There is no clear indication that Beowulf, though he has survived an additional half century of struggle, is essentially different from the young hero who went to help Hrothgar with the same motives. The dragon comes to Beowulf, to his people, to his own farm. Beowulf naturally speaks of the dragon's treasure as he prepares his comitatus for the journey, for he has seen the cup and has no knowledge of any curse upon the treasure. Yet he really has no choice but to go—he is the resident hero, and he is Beowulf. Our hero is mortally wounded fighting a dragon that he must fight, and the treasure business, however entrancing, is secondary. The poet uses it to develop the Christian theme of the worthlessness of worldly goods, and it indirectly brings about the downfall of his hero (because the wretched exile has stolen the dragon's cup and aroused his wrath), but surely there is no criticism of Beowulf himself here. When Beowulf is wounded and knows that he must die, naturally he wishes to see the treasure that he has won for his people; the thought of the riches will make leaving his responsibility to them easier to endure (lines 2747-51):

> "Bio nu on ofoste,   þæt ic ærwelan,
> goldæht ongite,   gearo sceawige
> swegle searogimmas,   þæt ic ðy seft mæge
> æfter maððumwelan   min alætan
> lif ond leodscipe,   þone ic longe heold."

(Hurry now that I may see the gold hoard, the ancient treasure, view eagerly the bright gems, so that I may more easily leave my life and kingship that I have held long.)

Where does cupidity come into this? Beowulf is dying—why not see the treasure? It is a part of the grim irony of the poet that the treasure avails Beowulf's people nought—but not, it should be noted, because they squander it and grow weak from luxury and misplaced values but because they choose to put it back into the earth, in Beowulf's barrow.[11] The fate that befalls Beowulf's people has nothing to do with the treasure (except in that the theft of the cup initiated the series of events), nor does Beowulf's own fate.

Larger and more practical concerns occupy our poet. We should recognize that more lines are spent on the matter of the faithless warriors than on anything to do with the treasure. Beowulf has spared his people one fate because man can, by his strength and the help of God, avert fate—temporarily. In his greatest triumph he has spared his people one sort of fate, but in his death he has, ironically, speeded them toward another. Perhaps this is what is meant by Wiglaf's gnomic comment about the choice of one man (lines 3077-78):

> "Oft sceall earl monig   anes willan
> wræc adreog*an*,   swa us geworden is."

(Oft shall many an earl endure misery through the choice of one, as has happened to us.)

But in any case we cannot see that he is referring to Beowulf's weakness for material possessions. Goldsmith would reply that all this is on the literal level, that her interpretation is the allegorical one. We will let her speak for herself:

> I would interpret the allegory like this: the rifling of the hoard, by exhibiting the dragon's costly cup to Beowulf and his men, lets loose the fiery breath of Leviathan through the

kingdom. Beowulf suffers unwonted disturbance of mind and a sense of estrangement from God. . . . He is enticed by thought of the treasure and the fame that will accrue to him if he wins it. His challenge to the dragon allegorically presents his attempts to repulse this thought, but he is already spiritually weakened by the feeling of self-sufficiency which long years of success have bred. Hence he goes into the fight foolishly trusting in his own strength, looking neither to man nor to God for help. He makes provision for the fight with a great iron shield, when what he needs is the shield of faith. On the historical level, this is simply making physical rather than spiritual preparation; allegorically, Beowulf's defence is his own justice. The iron (236) shield protects him all too short a time; what saves him from utter defeat is the intervention of Wiglaf.[12]

We will push our disagreement with Goldsmith no further than to observe that in the passage describing Beowulf's disturbance of mind Beowulf quite understandably wonders whether he has done something "ofer ealde riht" (against ancient law, line 2330a) to cause such a cataclysmic instance of God's displeasure. He looks back over his career—certainly an exemplary one in terms of both military glory and unparalleled morality; he has protected his people but sought no wars of conquest; he has refused even at the request of the queen to take over the kingship in place of her underage son; he has loyally served his lords; and so on. Contrary to Goldsmith's assertion, he nowhere speaks of seeking the fame that will come from the treasure; he thinks of it only as a good for his people, for he does not know about the curse. Surely the proper use of money is not frowned upon in the New Testament, and just as certainly the dispensing of gold is held in high regard among the peoples of our poem.

We feel finally that such criticism, however supported by

175

learned commentary, forever runs parallel with the events and language of the poem and nowhere meets them. This is the sort of thing that Sisam rightly condemns as speculation upon those things that are not *expressed* in *Beowulf.* We have chosen *The Mode and Meaning of Beowulf* for discussion as a type of recent criticism, not because the author's arguments fill us with more horror than those of other writers but because it is the most extensive example to date of this kind of approach. And it would be churlish not to express gratitude that Goldsmith's analysis specifically excludes an interpretation of Beowulf as Christ!

An interpretation as vigorous and dubious as Goldsmith's is advanced by Charles Donahue in "*Beowulf* and Christian Tradition: A Reconsideration from a Celtic Stance." Here the theological oddness of *Beowulf* is explained in light of the isolated Christian tradition in Britain and Ireland. For Donahue the allegory is more flexible than it is seen to be by others; Beowulf is to be equated with Christ only in the last part of the poem—earlier he is seen as first Abraham and then Job. The suggestion that Beowulf is to be equated typologically with Christ is not new, of course. The idealization of the hero in the poem moved many earlier scholars to the verge of the equation, most notably Klaeber.[13] But it is in more recent years that this interpretation has been pushed most vigorously.

Other ethical and semitheological interpretations have also been advanced, perhaps the most influential being the one by R. E. Kaske in his important "*Sapientia et Fortitudo* as the Controlling Theme of *Beowulf*" (1958). Kaske, as his title implies, sees the pagan-Christian ideal of the hero-king's wisdom and strength as underlying the poem not only in structure and characterization of a traditional sort but in the poet's deliberate didactic intent. *Beowulf* is for him a poem dealing explicitly with the working out of this theme. Although

Kaske asserts an allegorically inclined consciousness poet that we cannot subscribe to and insists upon ς application of the theme to episodes that seem to resist such interpretation, his analysis is generally illuminating and helpful and is, on the whole, the best of the allegorical interpretations.

In addition to Sisam's attack on the Christian-allegorical approaches to the poem, Charles Moorman published an article ("The Essential Paganism of *Beowulf*") emphasizing the slender factual basis for such top-heavy intellectual structure in *Beowulf*. But we feel that, like Sisam, he goes too far in his reaction and almost advocates a return to Blackburn's old monkish-interpolator view.

One can see that the present dominance of the Christian interpretations, allegorical or only semiallegorical, are direct responses to Tolkien's call (however distasteful he might find them) to understand the poem as a whole work. But many are very much in danger not of reading a whole poem but of confusing implications and assumed attitudes with poetic genius and mistaking one of the world's great poems for a philosophical or theological treatise.

The Oral-Formulaic Controversy

The third significant development in *Beowulf* criticism has been the rise of the "oral-formulaic" school, which we have already discussed in chapter 9. The impetus for this movement was provided in 1953 by F. P. Magoun, Jr., in "The Oral-Formulaic Character of Anglo-Saxon Narrative Poetry." His concept is simple. Basing his argument on the formulaic analyses of Milman Parry and Alfred B. Lord, who worked with Greek epic and Slavic oral poetry, Magoun argued that the high incidence of formulas in *Beowulf* warranted the conclusion not that *Beowulf* was composed in an oral tradition (that is, in an era of literacy in which the methods of writing poetry show strong traces of an earlier, nonliterate oral method of composition) but that it was itself actually composed orally, i.e., extemporaneously.[14] This idea, which Lord had put forth and subsequently restated in *The Singer of Tales,*[15] was developed by a number of other scholars, particularly R. P. Creed. After the first surge of enthusiasm, however, some scholars—H. L. Rogers and R. D. Stevick, to name but two—began to have doubts. The formulaic nature of Old English poetry—that is, its high percentage of repeated words, phrases, and even larger syntactical structures—had long been recognized, and the new interest in a particular interpretation of this evidence evoked considerable response. But as the implications began to become clearer, it was obvious that an approach to poetry that conceived its origins, in something like its present form, to have been oral and practically or specifically spontaneous, ran counter to a number of other critical preoccupations of this period. Those who wished to emphasize the close texture of the poem, the skillful foreshadowings, intricate allusions, and so on, found it difficult to accept the implications of oral composition. Thus Brodeur dismissed at once the idea of an unlettered poet composing *Beowulf* orally.[16] He is perfectly willing to accept the theory of a lettered poet composing within a tradition of oral poetry, with formulas that had their origins in an unlettered age, but argues strenuously throughout his book that the *Beowulf* poet was a lettered and probably a learned man. Likewise, Alistair Campbell, in his brief, brilliant "The Old English Epic Style," emphatically asserts a quality of Old English verse that could not, he argues, be compatible with oral compositon: "The carefully wrought paragraphs of the Old English epic style were certainly intended for preservation, and it follows that the poems were composed for record in writing."[17]

Such scholars as Malone and Bonjour have also rejected the basic oral-formulaic argument. William Whallon, in "The Diction of *Beowulf*," argued that *Beowulf*, even granting Magoun's assumptions, is very far from being totally formulaic. Like Brodeur, Larry Benson, in "The Literary Character of Anglo-Saxon Formulaic Poetry," argues that the oral composition of most surviving Anglo-Saxon poetry is improbable but that the formulaic quality that had marked a previous oral tradition could and did survive into an era of written poetry, contrary to one of Magoun's principal assumptions. Proponents of the oral-formulaic theory have attempted to demonstrate the wide range of devices available to the oral singer, which allow the modern critic to pass judgment on his literary skill rather than to assume that formulaic poetry is all of a piece, with little differentiation possible. Notably, R. P. Creed, in "On the Possibility of Criticizing Old English Poetry," and F. G. Cassidy, in "How Free Was the Anglo-Saxon Scop?" have concerned themselves with the questions of choice facing the presumed illiterate singer and have argued that he possessed the latitude that allowed for "good" and "bad" poetry as judged by any standard. But the brilliance of the *Beowulf* poet seems finally to elude their categories.

In the view of critics who assume careful written composition of *Beowulf*, the most damaging effect of a rigid application of oral-formulaic theory is Magoun's final thesis about *Beowulf*. Because of the theory that oral singers do not compose cyclic poems but sing episodically, Magoun is led by another route to return to the nineteenth-century theory that *Beowulf* consists of several parts composed by different singers. These, in subsequent articles, he has designated as *Beowulf A* (lines 1-2009a), *Beowulf A'* (lines 2009b-2176b), and *Beowulf B* (lines 2200-3182). As Magoun points out, such a theory "can in no way alter for better or worse the final effect achieved in the manuscript."[18] But the theory certainly runs counter to most of the modern assumptions about the structure of the poem and the presiding genius of a single poet. It is worth noting that, so far, Magoun's theory has not been enthusiastically embraced even by those who have heretofore fought by his side in the scholarly trenches.

Ann C. Watts, in *The Lyre and the Harp* (1969), has approached the subject of oral-formulaic composition from its inception and elaboration in the work of Milman Parry up to the present stage of the dispute. Watts traces step by step the gradual shifts in meaning and emphasis in the definition and application of the terms. She concludes that, while Magoun and his followers have made valuable contributions to our appreciation of Old English poetry, the theory has been distorted, misapplied, and pushed much too far: "On the one hand, Magoun and his followers, while professing to adopt, have not consistently adopted the major parts of Parry's thesis, or they have not explained or discussed those changes they thought must be made. Neither have they considered adequately the Homeric and Old English differences of language, time, and poetical form."[19] Certainly, she argues, there has been no convincing demonstration that *Beowulf* was composed orally. One feels that, with the inevitable sobering that must follow an enthusiasm, this conclusion is generally accepted at the present time, though all, or almost all, scholars would welcome a really convincing demonstration of the oral composition of *Beowulf* when and if it should occur.

In summarizing the critical trends of the past thirty years, we believe that, in spite of the controversies we have chronicled, scholars have moved to a position of fairly general agreement. The impetus given by Tolkien's lecture has pushed criticism to the point that it is now widely accepted (1) that *Beowulf,* as it stands, is the work of a single man of genius of a literate era, writing or composing within the modes of a previous and still-influential tradition of oral literary creation; (2) that this single man of genius was a Christian who consciously created his poem out of pagan materials; (3) that the resulting poem, while not an allegory, owes much of its intricate structure to a Christian view, as well as to the poet's knowledge of how to put together a long poem; and (4) that the resulting *Beowulf,* with its balances, its intricate weaving of themes, its diction strikingly original within a traditional frame, is one of the supreme creations of Anglo-Germanic literature. Most students of *Beowulf* would, we believe, subscribe more or less wholeheartedly to these conclusions. Although many corners of *Beowulf* have been illuminated since Tolkien's lecture, and our understanding of Anglo-Saxon poetry has advanced since that time, one may note with some awe that the conclusions above are still, in outline, those of Tolkien.

Interesting as all this criticism is, we should never allow ourselves to substitute the reading of criticism for reading and rereading the poem. Nor should we forget that a reading of other Old English literature and the study of Anglo-Saxon history and customs may be more profitable than an immersion in criticism to the exclusion of primary sources. For, by acquainting ourselves with Anglo-Saxon culture, we at least dimly become one of the *Beowulf* poet's nearer audience, more actively participating in that poet's achievement. But even without making much of an effort, among generations of students few have failed to be moved by the vigor, power, and simple heroic vision of the poet, whose gift of weaving words and creating scenes and speeches that haunt the imagination has given us a poem that with all its "barbaric" qualities lies beyond the power of scholars and critics to recapture or to explain.

181

Abbreviations Used in
Notes and Bibliography

For full citations, see Annotated Bibliography.

ABC	Lewis E. Nicholson, ed., *An Anthology of Beowulf Criticism*
ALLCJ	*Association for Literary and Linguistic Computing Journal*
ASE	*Anglo-Saxon England*
BGDSL	*Beiträge zur Geschichte der deutschen Sprache und Literatur*
BP	Donald K. Fry, ed., *The Beowulf Poet*
C&M	*Classica et Mediaevalia*
EA	Jess B. Bessinger, Jr., and Stanley J. Kahrl, eds., *Essential Articles for the Study of Old English Poetry*
EETS	Early English Text Society
ELH	*Journal of English Literary History*
ES	*English Studies*
JEGP	*Journal of English and Germanic Philology*
MÆ	*Medium Ævum*

MHRA	Modern Humanities Research Association
MLQ	*Modern Language Quarterly*
MP	*Modern Philology*
Neophil	*Neophilologus*
NM	*Neuphilologische Mitteilungen*
OEP	R. P. Creed, ed., *Old English Poetry: Fifteen Essays*
PBA	*Proceedings of the British Academy*
PMLA	*PMLA: Publications of the Modern Language Association of America*
RES	*Review of English Studies*
SP	*Studies in Philology*
TSLL	*Texas Studies in Literature and Language*
UTQ	*University of Toronto Quarterly*

Notes

CHAPTER 1

1. Late medieval and early Renaissance libraries usually catalogued books by bookcase, shelf, and number on shelf (e.g., Cambridge University Library (Gg. v.35). In the Cottonian Library, cases were desnated not by number or letter but by the busts of famous persons of antiquity that stood on them; hence Cotton Vitellius A.15. As larger collections grew up, books were given their numbers in the original collections that had been absorbed: Oxford, Bodleian, Junius 11; British Museum, Harleian, 213. Later, Bodleian and some other manuscripts were given sequential numbers, but many books are still known by their original designation, sometimes with the later number given in parentheses: Junius 11 (5123).

2. In most early manuscripts, leaves (folios) rather than pages were numbered. "Recto," abbreviated as a lowercase *r*, indicates the front of a folio; *verso* — *v* — indicates the back.

CHAPTER 2

1. For a discussion of the performance of poets and appropriate lengths of song story, see Alfred B. Lord, *The Singer of Tales*, pp. 13-29, 99-123, especially "Some Notes on Medieval Epic," pp. 198-221. We do not agree with some of Lord's conclusions, specifically his certainty that *Beowulf* was composed orally, but there is no doubt that his analysis of the work of Balkan oral poets throws some light on the function of such persons in Anglo-Saxon courts. The methodological basis of the work of Lord and of Milman Parry, however, has been sharply called into question by several scholars, most re-

cently by Rudy Spraycar, in "Automatic Lemmatization in Serbo-Croatian," *ALLCJ* 1 (1980):55-59.

CHAPTER 3

1. Colin Chase has edited a volume of essays, *The Dating of Beowulf,* on this vexed question.

2. Sutton Hoo is a mound in Essex that contained a seventh-century ship burial. Fortunately spared from plundering by early grave robbers, it was scientifically excavated from 1939 onward. It contained a magnificent collection of armor and barbarian jewelry. Perhaps the best way to appreciate at secondhand the beauty of the gold-and-garnet work in the collection, at the British Museum, is in the color slides of the British Museum. A more extensive presentation of the material, with comment, appears in R. L. S. Bruce-Mitford, *The Sutton Hoo Ship-Burial: A Handbook,* first issued by the British Museum in 1968 and updated from time to time. See also Bruce-Mitford's appendix, "The Sutton Hoo Ship-Burial," in R. H. Hodgkin, *A History of the Anglo-Saxons,* 3d ed., 2:676-734; and Charles L. Wrenn, "Sutton Hoo and *Beowulf,*" in *Mélanges de linguistique et de philologie in Memoriam Fernand Mossé.*

3. We are not certain whether any of the tribes that appear in early Scandinavian history was the Geats. Consequently, some points in Swedish-Geatish relations are uncertain. We do know, however, that the Geats harbored Swedish refugees (*Beowulf,* lines 2202-2206, 2390-96) and intervened in Swedish civil wars (lines 2472-89, 2610-19, 2922-88). No doubt the Swedes behaved similarly on occasion. Presumably the two kingdoms were close together, and many scholars consider that the Gautar of southern Sweden were the Geats (see map on p. viii of Klaeber's edition of *Beowulf*). Some have suggested that the Jutes, one of the tribes that invaded Britain after the collapse of Rome, were the Geats, and, to complicate matters, some have tried to identify the Jutes with the Gautar. Fortunately, the reader of *Beowulf* does not have to worry about the identity of the Geats unless he wants to.

4. Kenneth Hurlstone Jackson, *The Oldest Irish Tradition: A Window on the Iron Age,* Rede Lecture (Cambridge: Cambridge Uni-

versity Press, 1964), pp. 24-26: "Incidentally, I might mention, as pure *obiter dictum,* that although Irish poets were able to recite orally an impressive amount of verse, they did not do so by improvisation." Apprentice bards composed by a method strikingly like that attributed to Caedmon by Bede (*Historia ecclesiastica* 4.22.[24]): "... the teacher ... set subjects for composition, which was done by pupils *in their heads* [italics ours] lying on their beds in the dark." It should be noted, incidentally, that the ability to recite verse from memory and the ability to compose extemporaneously (as the English almost certainly did on occasion) are not mutually exclusive.

CHAPTER 4

1. Ælfric's homily is 1.4 in Thorpe's edition, *The Sermones Catholici, or Homilies of Aelfric,* 2 vols. (Aelfric Society, 1844-46). Many of us know it because it is included in Bright's *Anglo-Saxon Reader.* It is item 6, fols. 13-17, in Cambridge University Library MS Gg. 3.28, incipit "Iohannes se godspellere cristes dyrling.

2. Dorothy Whitelock, *The Audience of Beowulf,* pp. 13-19.

3. Ibid., pp. 12, 82-85.

4. For a full discussion of Alfred's views, see F. Anne Payne, *King Alfred and Boethius* (Madison: University of Wisconsin Press, 1968), pp. 68ff. References to Alfred in the text are to Walter John Sedgefield, *King Alfred's Old English Version of Boethius* (1899; reprint, Darmstadt: Wissenschaftliche Buchgesellschaft, 1968). Our citations have contractions expanded and parentheses omitted. An approach to the understanding of *Beowulf* by attempting to view the poem through the eyes of a possible contemporary, Alcuin, is the theme of W. F. Bolton, *Alcuin and Beowulf: An Eighth-Century View.* The narrowly intellectual vision is not, however, very convincing (see review by T. A. Shippey in *MÆ* 49 [1980]:268-71).

5. Payne, *King Alfred and Boethius,* pp. 48-50.

CHAPTER 5

1. According to Lucy Kavalar, *Mushrooms, Molds, and Miracles* (New York: John Day, 1965), p. 162, the berserk state was probably induced by eating the mushroom *Amanita muscaria.*

CHAPTER 6

1. For an excellent statement on these points, see Kemp Malone, "Beowulf the Headstrong," *ASE 1* (1972):139-45. Malone writes:

"What of the advice Beowulf got from Wiglaf and his fellows [to leave the dragon alone]? If the king had agreed to do nothing, would his subjects have been better off? Obviously he would be leaving them (and himself) at the mercy of the dragon, and the dragon was not merciful. . . .

"The epithet *folces weard* [guardian of the people] which the hero gives himself at this crisis in his people's story shows what he is doing when he takes his stand against the dragon. As Klaeber puts it, Beowulf 'undertakes the venture primarily to save his people.' . . .

"Glory and booty will come to the hero if he wins the dragon fight and he is mindful of both (2514a and 2536a); hence Klaeber's 'primarily.' One must agree with Klaeber that these fruits of victory are secondary for Beowulf, who is first of all the king, the *folces weard.* They are of course conventional rewards for the hero of a dragon fight in popular story, and it would have been remiss of the poet to make his hero indifferent to either one. . . .

"Under Beowulf the Geats lived in peace and freedom; after his death the Geatish state fell, victim of attacks from abroad. The contrast serves, of course, to exalt the hero. . . . But . . . it would hold good whether Beowulf died of a dragon's bite a little sooner or of old age a little later. . . .

"Many great men have died in bed, but for heroic story Beowulf's way of dying is as it should be. . . . Beowulf dies as he had lived, a *folces weard.*"

Considering that our chapter and Malone's article were written altogether independently of each other, their agreement is striking.

2. Fafnir was a man transformed into a dragon (see *Reginsmol* sec. 14, prose, in *The Elder Edda*). In the most ancient known dragon story also, the Sumerian hero Gilgamesh and the dragon Huwawa converse. See Samuel N. Kramer, *History Begins at Sumer* (Garden City, N.Y.: Doubleday, Anchor Books, 1959), pp. 174-81.

3. Only the Geats avoided this practice; see the statement on the

loyalty of Beowulf and Hygelac to each other (lines 2169-71). Unferth had killed his brothers (lines 587-88, 1167-68). In the tale of Finnsburg, uncle and nephew, who had died fighting on opposite sides, were burned on the same pyre (lines 1114-16). The feuds and killings among members of the Swedish royal family occupy a considerable place in the second part of *Beowulf* (lines 2472-89, 2612-19, 2922-98). See also pp. xliv-xlv in Klaeber's introduction to his edition of *Beowulf*.

A feeling of impending disaster for the Danish royal house permeates the first part of *Beowulf;* yet only two short passages—we might almost say only two words—refer to the coming doom of the Scyldings. Some of this sense may arise from facts known to the poet and his audience, and to us, but not stated in the poem. Lines 1017-19 read: "All within Heorot was filled with friends. By no means did the Scylding yet [þenden] practice treachery." In lines 1163-65 we find: "There the two good ones sat, nephew and paternal uncle [Hrothulf and Hrothgar]; yet was their peace unbroken; each was true to the other." The implication is that this state of affairs is not destined to endure. The following lines (1165-68) show Unferth sitting at the feet of Hrothgar and tell us that both Hrothgar and Hrothulf have confidence in him. The worried tone of Wealtheow's speech (lines 1169-87) adds to the general sense of foreboding that begins with lines 81-85: "The hall towered, high and horn-gabled, awaited the battle surges of the hostile flame. Nor was it long until the sword hate of son- and father-in-law should awaken after deadly hatred." The reference is to the burning of Heorot in the Heatho-Bard feud, which is outside the events of *Beowulf*. The actual cause of the conflict in which Heorot was destroyed is something of a mystery (see Raymond W. Chambers, *Beowulf: An Introduction to the Study of the Poem,* 3d ed., pp. 13-31), but clearly the poet intends to suggest that the slaughter of kinsmen is involved. Slaughter of kinsmen was abhorrent but much indulged in; most of the great Germanic heroes were stained with it, including Sigmund, Gunnar, Hogni, Hildebrand, Hæthcyn, Hnæf, and Eadgils. That so monumental a figure as Beowulf should be unmarred by such a defect impresses us further with the uniqueness of our hero.

4. H. M. Smyser, "Ibn Fadlān's Account of the Rus," in Jess B.

Bessinger, Jr., and Robert P. Creed, eds., *Franciplegius* (New York: New York University Press, 1965), pp. 92-119. Compare also the Celtic tradition of "keening."

CHAPTER 7

1. British Library Cotton Caligula A.7, with Latin glosses in an English hand.
2. Kemp Malone, "The Daughter of Healfdene," in S. Einarsson and N. E. Eliason, eds., *Studies in Heroic Legend and in Current Speech*, p. 127 (reprinted from *Studies in English Philology: A Miscellany in Honor of Frederick Klaeber* (Minneapolis: University of Minnesota Press, 1929), pp. 135-58).
3. Charles Plummer, ed., *The Anglo-Saxon Chronicle*, pp. 90-91.
4. Ibid., pp. 47-49.
5. Bede *Historia ecclesiastica* 2.9, in Charles Plummer, ed., *Bedae opera historica* (Oxford: Oxford University Press, 1896), 1:98-99.
6. H. R. E. Davidson, *The Sword in Anglo-Saxon England* (Oxford: Clarendon Press, 1962), p. 159. In *Thithriks Saga* (thirteenth century but based on older sources), Nægling appears with two other legendary swords, Mimming and Ekisax.
7. Such a standard, or "tufa," is well illustrated in the bronze stag of the Sutton Hoo find; photographs of the stag and of the reconstructed standard, or "segn," as it was also known (see *Beowulf*, lines 2767, 2776), appear in plate 2 of R. L. S. Bruce-Mitford, *The Sutton Hoo Ship-Burial: A Handbook.* See our drawing of the stag.
8. Bede *Historia ecclesiastica* 3.12, in Plummer, ed., *Bedae opera historica*, 1:151.
9. The English defeats noted among the eight *folc gefeoht* in the *Anglo-Saxon Chronicle* under the year 871 were drawn battles in which one side or the other might drive the enemy from the field, but the defeated host remained an army in being, as the short intervals between battles attest, so that they are not exceptions to this rule.
10. On the prevalence of the blood feud in Christian England down to 1066, see Dorothy Whitelock, *The Audience of Beowulf,* pp. 13-19.

CHAPTER 8

1. Perhaps the most important of Sievers's early works is "Zur Rhythmik des germanischen Alliterationverses I," *BGDSL* 10 (1885): 209-314.

2. *Beowulf* contains eleven lines (1163-68, 1705-1707, 2995-96), ranging in length from twelve to eighteen syllables, which Sievers could not fit into his Five Types classification. These have been called for obvious reasons "hypermetrical." Actually, the interesting point about them is not their length, for "ordinary" lines frequently have twelve or thirteen or even fifteen syllables, but their appearance in groups, with the result that their peculiarity is striking. For an elaborate discussion, see John C. Pope's treatment in *The Rhythm of Beowulf*, pp. 99-156.

3. Paull Baum, "The Meter of the 'Beowulf,'" *MP* 46 (1948-49):73-91, 145-62.

4. Max Kaluza, *Der Altenglische Vers: Eine metrische Untersuchung* (Berlin, 1894).

5. A. J. Bliss, *The Metre of Beowulf*.

6. Edouard Sievers, "Zu Cynewulf," *Neusprachliche Studien: Festgabe für Karl Luick (Die Neueren Sprachen)* 33, 6 (1925):60-81.

7. Andreas Heusler, *Deutsche Versgeschichte, mit Einschluss des altenglischen und altnordischen Stabreimverses*.

8. Pope, *The Rhythm of Beowulf.*

9. William Thomson, *The Rhythm of Speech* (Glasgow, 1923).

10. Pope, *The Rhythm of Beowulf*, p. 90.

11. Bliss, *The Metre of Beowulf*, p. 2.

12. Baum, "The Meter of the 'Beowulf.'" Jane-Marie Luecke, in *Measuring Old English Rhythm: An Application of the Principles of Gregorian Chant Rhythm to the Meter of "Beowulf,"* attempts to show a real influence of Gregorian chant (not Baum's argument) but in our opinion is unsuccessful. See a review of her work by A. J. Bliss in *MÆ* 49 (1980):274-75.

13. Pope, *The Rhythm of Beowulf*, p. x.

14. See Baum, "The Meter of the 'Beowulf,'" p. 75; J. W. Rankin, "Rhythm and Rime Before the Norman Conquest," *PMLA* 36 (1921):

401-28. See also Jess B. Bessinger, Jr., "The Sutton Hoo Harp Replica and Old English Musical Verse," in *OEP,* pp. 3-26. Bessinger favors Pope's theory but presents a fair assessment of the evidence.

15. Joseph Taglicht, "*Beowulf* and Old English Verse Rhythm," *RES,* n.s. 12 (1961):341-51.

16. Pope, *The Rhythm of Beowulf,* p. lx.

17. Robert P. Creed, "The Rhythm of 'Beowulf,'" *PMLA* 81 (1966): 23-33.

18. John Nist, "Metrical Uses of the Harp in *Beowulf,*" in *OEP,* pp. 27-43.

19. Ibid., p. 32.

20. Ibid.

21. Ibid., p. 34.

22. Pope, *The Rhythm of Beowulf,* p. 41.

23. Baum, "The Meter of the 'Beowulf,'" p. 146.

24. O. F. Emerson, "Transverse Alliteration in Teutonic Poetry, *JEGP* 3 (1900):127-37.

25. There are some lines that defy the reader to achieve a time balance between the verses, e.g., line 862: "Ne hie huru winedrihten wiht ne logon." To balance these verses would require a rest of Gargantuan proportions or a mightily reverberating harp stroke. Since the grammatical and rhetorical links of the verses are immediate—and there is no emphatic break between the a and b verses—the clear course would appear to be to admit that the verses are not equal or to claim that the first verse contains a prodigious anacrusis.

26. Frederick Klaeber, ed., *Beowulf and The Fight at Finnsburg,* 3d ed., p. 281; Bliss, *The Metre of Beowulf,* pp. 139-67.

27. J. R. R. Tolkien, "Prefatory Remarks," in *Beowulf and the Finnsburg Fragment,* trans. J. R. Clark Hall, pp. ix-xliii.

CHAPTER 9

1. Francis P. Magoun, Jr., "The Oral Formulaic Character of Anglo-Saxon Poetry," *Speculum* 28 (1952):446-67.

2. For a variety of approaches to the evidence on this question, the student should consult the works by Benson, Creed, Greenfield, Lord, Magoun, Watt, and Whallon listed in the Bibliography. We

discuss something of the course of this controversy in chapter 10. At the core of the problem is the question whether the characteristics of the oral formula that Milman Parry and Alfred B. Lord observed in twentieth-century Balkan poetry composed orally and that they also find in the poetry of the *Iliad* and the *Odyssey* are also those of the formula of Germanic poetry. The scholarly consensus at present is that they are not. The syllabic regularity of Greek meter, on which Parry's concept of the oral formula is based, has no parallel in Germanic poetry. The far greater variety of formulaic epithet found in *Beowulf,* which admits of far more specific appropriateness to context, sets it apart from the more rigidly stereotyped Greek epithet. It would be fair to say that, although every scholar today would assume that the formulaic qualities of Old English are of a kind that has its origin in nonliterate poetry—i.e., a poetry not only orally transmitted but orally created—the great majority of scholars would maintain that *Beowulf*'s enormous variety of epithet would in itself likely preclude oral composition of the poem.

3. It is beyond our brief to argue here whether we ought to label as kennings many of the Old English figures usually so called. For the technically accurate claim that most are *kend heiti,* see the discussion by Arthur G. Brodeur in *The Art of Beowulf,* p. 18.

4. For illustration of the variation of which the *Beowulf* poet was capable, see the discussion in ibid. and the appendix of epithets unique to *Beowulf.*

5. For a thorough comparison of the Anglo-Saxon and the Homeric epithet, see William Whallon, *Formula, Character, and Context: Studies in Homeric, Old English, and Old Testament Poetry.*

6. G. P. Krapp, ed., *The Vercelli Book,* in *The Anglo-Saxon Poetic Records,* vol. 2. (New York: Columbia University Press, 1932), p. 51.

7. Ibid., p. 3.

8. Bruce Dickins and A. S. C. Ross, eds., *The Dream of the Rood* (London: Methvem, 1934), p. 20.

9. See discussions of this theme in F. P. Magoun, Jr., "The Theme of the Beasts of Battle in Anglo-Saxon Poetry," *NM* 56 (1955): 81-90; and Adrian Bonjour, "*Beowulf* and the Beasts of Battle," in his *Twelve Beowulf Papers,* pp. 135-46.

10. E. V. K. Dobbie, ed., *The Anglo-Saxon Minor Poems,* in *The Anglo-Saxon Poetic Records,* vol. 6 (New York: Columbia University Press, 1942), pp. 19-20.

11. See chapter 7 for discussion of these themes.

12. J. R. R. Tolkien, "Prefatory Remarks," in J. R. Clark Hall, trans., *Beowulf and the Finnsburg Fragment,* p. xliii.

13. Such is the underlying assumption of Kenneth Sisam in *The Structure of Beowulf.*

14. For a stimulating discussion of the poet's uses of repetition and variation, the reader is referred to Arthur G. Brodeur, *The Art of Beowulf,* pp. 39-70. See our remarks on Brodeur's arguments in chapter 10.

CHAPTER 10

1. Arthur G. Brodeur, *The Art of Beowulf,* p. 87.

2. John Leyerle, "Beowulf the Hero and the King," *MÆ* 34 (1965):89.

3. H. G. Wright, "Good and Evil; Light and Darkness; Joy and Sorrow in Beowulf," *RES,* n.s., 8 (1957):11.

4. One of the present authors has also aired his views on this subject; see J. D. A. Ogilvy, "Unferth: Foil to Beowulf?" *PMLA* 79 (1964):370-75.

5. Of course, the poet has explicitly told us that Unferth in his newfound admiration of Beowulf and his recognition of his own inability does not bear in mind now those things that he had spoken earlier (lines 1465-1468a):

> Huru ne gemunde   mago Ecglafes
> eafopes cræftig,   þæt he ær gespræc
> wine druncen,   þa he þæs wæpnes onlah
> selran sweordfrecan;

(Indeed, the kinsman of Ecglaf did not now bear in mind, that one powerful in his strength, the things that he had earlier spoken, flown with wine, when he lent the weapon to the better warrior;)

Clearly, either the poet is misleading or Rosier is.

6. Kenneth Sisam, *The Structure of Beowulf,* p. 21.

7. Ibid., p. 27.

8. Ibid., p. 78, note B.

9. Dorothy Whitelock, *The Audience of Beowulf,* p. 3.

10. Kenneth Sisam, *Studies in the History of Old English Literature,* p. 66.

11. The poet actually seems to think that such a disposition of the treasure is a waste, contrary to Goldsmith's assumptions about his attitude; see lines 3166-68. It is interesting to compare Beowulf's "cupidity" with that of Wilfrid of York, called by R. H. Hodgkins (*A History of the Anglo-Saxons,* 1:346) "*miles* Christi" (warrior of Christ), who surveyed his hoard of treasure before his death and ordered it divided for the use of the church, as described by his biographer Eddius.

12. M. E. Goldsmith, *The Mode and Meaning of Beowulf,* pp. 235-36.

13. Frederick Klaeber, ed., *Beowulf and The Fight at Finnsburg,* p. li.

14. Magoun, "The Oral-Formulaic Character of Anglo-Saxon Poetry." *Speculum,* 28 (1953).

15. Alfred B. Lord, *The Singer of Tales,* pp. 198-202.

16. Arthur G. Brodeur, *The Art of Beowulf,* p. 4.

17. Alistair Campbell, "The Old English Epic Style," in N. Davis and C. L. Wrenn, eds., *English and Medieval Studies Presented to J. R. R. Tolkien,* p. 20.

18. F. P. Magoun, Jr., "*Beowulf B:* A Folk-Poem on Beowulf's Death," in A. Brown and P. Foote, eds., *Early English and Norse Studies Presented to Hugh Smith,* p. 127.

19. Ann C. Watts, *The Lyre and the Harp,* p. 195.

Annotated Bibliography

This is a select bibliography, the critical items especially having been chosen to illustrate as widely as possible the range of approaches to *Beowulf.* No effort at comprehensiveness has been made, nor all the entries discussed in the text.

Editions of Beowulf

Dobbie, E. van K., ed. *Beowulf and Judith.* Vol. 4 in *The Anglo-Saxon Poetic Records.* New York: Columbia University Press, 1953. In standard series with the corpus of Old English poetry. Moderately conservative text with full textual notes but little commentary.

Klaeber, Frederick, ed. *Beowulf and The Fight at Finnsburg.* 3d ed. New York: D. C. Heath, 1941; reprint with first and second supplements, 1950. Still the best school edition, with elaborate apparatus.

Wrenn, Charles L., ed. *Beowulf and the Finnsburg Fragment.* 2d ed. London: C. G. Harrap, 1958. 3d ed., revised by W. F. Bolton, 1973. Fine school edition, conservative; Bolton restores the manuscript's contracted forms that Wrenn had expanded.

Wyatt, A. J., ed. *Beowulf with the Finnsburg Fragment.* New ed., revised by R. W. Chambers. Cambridge: Cambridge University Press, 1914. 2d ed., 1920; reprint, 1968. Very conservative text, excellent discussions by Chambers.

Facsimiles

Malone, Kemp, ed. *The Nowell Codex*. Vol. 12 in *Early English Manuscripts in Facsimile*. Copenhagen: Rosenkilde and Bagger, 1963. New photographs of the manuscript with elaborate commentary.

Zupitza, Julius, ed. *Beowulf*. EETS, o.s., vol. 77. Oxford: Oxford University Press, 1882. 2d ed., edited by Norman Davis. EETS, o.s., vol. 245. Oxford: Oxford University Press, 1959. In the 1959 edition the facsimiles are new, though Zupitza's transliteration and notes are retained.

Concordance

Bessinger, Jess B., Jr., and P. H. Smith, Jr., eds. *A Concordance to Beowulf*. Ithaca, N.Y.: Cornell University Press, 1969. A computer-assisted work that has replaced Albert S. Cook's *A Concordance to Beowulf* (1911).

Translations

Bradley, S. A. J., ed. and trans. *Anglo-Saxon Poetry*. Everyman's Library. London: J. M. Dent & Sons, 1982. An even more comprehensive collection of Anglo-Saxon poetry than Gordon's, below, which it is replacing in the Everyman's Library series.

Chickering, Howell D., Jr., trans. *Beowulf: A Dual Language Edition*. New York: Anchor Books, 1977. An extremely useful facing-text translation. The translation is broken into Anglo-Saxon half lines as closely as possible, and alliterative linkage is attempted. The imaginative and provocative introduction should appeal to all beginning students.

Donaldson, E. T., trans. *Beowulf: A New Prose Translation*. New York: W. W. Norton, 1966. An impressive version, after one recovers from the shock of finding the initial "Hwæt!" translated primly as "Yes."

Gordon, R. K., trans. *Anglo-Saxon Poetry.* Everyman's Library. London: E. P. Dent, 1926. A prose translation of the corpus of Anglo-Saxon poetry that is not as bad as some detractors say. It remains invaluable to the student.

Hall, J. R. Clark, trans. *Beowulf and the Finnsburg Fragment.* Rev. ed., with "Prefatory Remarks" by J. R. R. Tolkien, and Introduction by C. L. Wrenn. London: G. Allen and Unwin, 1950. Still a good translation, and Tolkien's comments on *Beowulf*'s meter are among the most helpful ever written.

Kennedy, C. W. *Beowulf: the Oldest English Epic.* New York: Oxford University Press, 1940. The best verse translation.

Bibliography

Fry, Donald K. *Beowulf and The Fight at Finnsburg: A Bibliography.* Charlottesville, Va.: University Press of Virginia, 1969. Attempts to include all work published to July, 1967. A useful system of subject classification, alphabetized by author, with a key to articles and books in which individual lines are discussed.

Greenfield, S., and F. C. Robinson. *A Bibliography of Publications on Old English to the End of 1972.* Toronto: University of Toronto Press, 1980.

Tinker, C. B. *The Translations of Beowulf: A Critical Bibliography.* With updating Bibliography by Marijane Osborn, new Foreword by F. C. Robinson. Hamden, Conn.: Archon, 1974. A useful tool for all students of the poem.

See *Old English Newsletter* for bibliography from 1967 onward.

Historical Background

Bolton, W. F. *Alcuin and Beowulf: An Eighth-Century View.* New Brunswick, N.J.: Rutgers University Press, 1978. Bolton focuses on the poem as Alcuin might have interpreted it.

Bruce-Mitford, R. L. S. *The Sutton Hoo Ship-Burial: A Handbook.* London: Trustees of the British Museum, 1968. An excellent survey of the most important Anglo-Saxon archaeological find.

Brunner, Karl. "Why was *Beowulf* Preserved?" *Études anglaises* 7 (1954):1-5.

Chadwick, H. Munro. *The Heroic Age.* Cambridge: Cambridge University Press, 1912. An excerpt from this vigorous survey is reprinted in *ABC.*

————, and Nora K. Chadwick. *The Ancient Literature of Europe.* Vol. 1 in *The Growth of Literature.* Cambridge: Cambridge University Press, 1932; reprint, 1968. Still a fascinating grab bag of information on heroic literature.

Chambers, Raymond W. *Beowulf: An Introduction to the Study of the Poem.* 3d ed. Supplement by C. L. Wrenn. Cambridge: Cambridge University Press, 1963. The most valuable book for the background of the poem.

————. *Widsith: A Study in Old English Heroic Legend.* Cambridge: Cambridge University Press, 1912; reprint, 1965. A splendid treatment of a type of legend that is used in *Beowulf.*

Chase, Colin, ed. *The Dating of Beowulf.* Toronto: University of Toronto Press, 1981. Essays by various scholars treating aspects of the problem of dating.

Cramp, Rosemary. "*Beowulf* and Archeology." *Medieval Archeology* 1 (1957): 57-77. Reprinted in *BP.* Stimulating application to the poem of new knowledge of custom, decoration, and architecture.

Garmonsway, G., and J. Simpson, trans. *Beowulf and Its Analogues.* Including "Archaeology and *Beowulf,*" by H. E. Davidson. London: J. M. Dent & Sons, 1980. First published in 1968. Includes all the parallels to the *Beowulf* material, good introductions, and Davidson's most valuable piece.

Girvan, R. *Beowulf and the Seventh Century.* London: Methuen & Co., 1935; reprint, 1971, with an additional chapter by R. L. S. Bruce-Mitford on the discoveries at Sutton Hoo.

Hodgkin, R. H. *A History of the Anglo-Saxons.* 3d ed. 2 vols.

Oxford: Oxford University Press, 1953. Still useful.

Kiernan, K. *Beowulf and the Beowulf Manuscript.* New Brunswick, N.J.: Rutgers University Press, 1982. A close analysis of Cotton Vitellius A.15, arguing that the poem and the manuscript may be contemporary.

Lawrence, W. W. *Beowulf and Epic Tradition.* Cambridge, Mass.: Harvard University Press, 1928; reprint, New York: Hafner, 1967.

Malone, Kemp. "The Tale of Ingeld." In S. Einarsson and N. E. Eliason, eds. *Studies in Heroic Legend and in Current Speech.* Copenhagen: Rosenkilde and Bagger, 1959, pp. 1–62. An exhaustive examination of one of the legends that appear in *Beowulf.*

Payne, F. Anne. "Three Aspects of Wyrd in *Beowulf.*" In R. B. Burlin and E. B. Irving, Jr., eds. *Old English Studies in Honour of John C. Pope.* Toronto: University of Toronto Press, 1974, pp. 15-35. Argues that *wyrd* is "the weight man's noblest efforts are anchored to" (p. 34) and is all that gives him freedom.

Plummer, Charles, ed. *The Anglo-Saxon Chronicle.* 2 vols. Oxford: Oxford University Press, 1892, 1899; reprint, 1952. The standard edition.

Sisam, Kenneth. *Studies in the History of Old English Literature.* Oxford: Oxford University Press, 1953. Contains an excellent treatment of the *Beowulf* manuscript.

Smithers, G. V. *The Making of Beowulf.* Durham: University of Durham, 1961. A comparison of *Beowulf* with other Germanic material using a similar central story.

Stenton, F. W. *Anglo-Saxon England.* 2d ed. Oxford: Oxford University Press, 1947. The best history of the period.

Whitelock, Dorothy, ed., with D. C. Douglas and S. I. Tucker. *The Anglo-Saxon Chronicle.* London: Eyre and Spottiswood, 1961. A revised translation with helpful notes.

———. *The Audience of Beowulf.* Oxford: Clarendon Press, 1951. The best of the chiefly historical studies of the poem to appear in the past several decades.

Wrenn, Charles L. "Sutton Hoo and Beowulf." In *Mélanges de*

linguistique et de philologie in memoriam Fernand Mossé.
Paris: Didier, 1959. Reprinted in *ABC.* An excellent brief
discussion of the implications of archaeological findings for
our understanding of the poem.

Versification and Poetics

Bartlett, Adeline C. *The Larger Rhetorical Patterns in Anglo-
Saxon Poetry.* New York: Columbia University Press, 1935.
A useful introduction to the subject. Although this study is
seldom acknowledged, much later study of style is in Bartlett's debt.

Baum, Paull F. "The Meter of the 'Beowulf.'" *MP* 46 (1948):
73-91, and (1949):145-62. An interesting corrective to overly
rigid systems of analysis, whether of the Sievers or of the
Pope schools.

Benson, Larry D. "The Literary Character of Anglo-Saxon Formulaic Poetry." *PMLA* 81 (1966):334-41. A nondogmatic study
drawing a suggestive parallel between the variations available
to the Anglo-Saxon poet and the neoclassical poet of the eighteenth century.

Bliss, A. J. *The Metre of Beowulf.* Oxford: B. H. Blackwell,
1958; revised and reprinted, 1962. A comprehensive restate-
ment of Sievers.

Burchfield, R. W. "The Prosodic Terminology of Anglo-Saxon
Scholars." In R. R. Burlin and Edward B. Irving, Jr., eds.
Old English Studies in Honour of John C. Pope. Toronto:
University of Toronto Press, 1974, pp. 171-202. A useful
guide to understanding what scholars mean or appear to mean
when they use prosodic terms in discussing Old English.

Cable, Thomas. *The Meter and Melody of Beowulf.* Urbana, Ill.:
University of Illinois Press, 1974. Considers the melodic, not
rhythmic, aspects of *Beowulf*'s music. Highly speculative but
provocative.

———. "Parallels to the Melodical Formulas of *Beowulf.*" *MP*

73 (1975):1-14. Finds Gregorian, Byzantine, and ancient Greek parallels for the melodic theories described in his *The Meter and Melody of Beowulf* (above).

Calder, Daniel G. "The Study of Style in Old English Poetry: A Historical Introduction." In Daniel G. Calder, ed. *Old English Poetry: Essays on Style.* Berkeley: University of California Press, 1979, pp. 1-65. A good place to start for anyone trying to grasp the background of our "understanding" of style.

Campbell, Alistair. "The Old English Epic Style." In N. Davis and Charles L. Wrenn, eds. *English and Medieval Studies Presented to J. R. R. Tolkien.* London: G. Allen and Unwin, 1962. An excellent brief essay that assumes a literate poem and poet.

Cassidy, F. G. "How Free Was the Anglo-Saxon Scop?" In Jess B. Bessinger, Jr., and Robert P. Creed, eds. *Franciplegius.* New York: New York University Press, 1965, pp. 75-85. Cassidy argues for considerable freedom within the apparently confined choices imposed on the scop by the oral-formulaic method.

Creed, Robert P. "The Making of an Anglo-Saxon Poem." *ELH* 26 (1959):445-54. Reprinted in *BP, EA,* and *OEL.* An attempt to reconstruct the process of creation in a few lines of *Beowulf.*

———. "A New Approach to the Rhythm of 'Beowulf.'" *PMLA* 80 (1966):23-33. Essentially a simplification of the theory of John C. Pope.

———. "On the Possibility of Criticizing Old English Poetry." *TSLL* 3 (1961):97-106. Deals, not too satisfactorily, with the basic *literary* problem confronting a committed believer in the oral-formulaic theory.

Diamond, R. E. "Theme as Ornament in Anglo-Saxon Poetry." *PMLA* 76 (1961):461-68. Reprinted in *EA* and in *BP.* A brief study of several Old English set themes and the extent and effect of their use.

Fry, Donald K. "Old English Formulas and Systems." *ES* 48 (1967):194-204. Attempts a redefinition of the formula, concluding that it is "a group of words, one-half line in length, which shows evidence of being the direct product of a formulaic system" (p. 204).

———, ed. *The Beowulf Poet*. Englewood Cliffs, N.J.: Prentice-Hall, 1968. A well-selected collection of standard pieces that provides something on every subject. Abbreviated *BP*.

———. "Variation and Economy in *Beowulf.*" *MP* 65 (1967-68): 353-56. Argues that variation is more characteristic of *Beowulf* than the economy that Milman Parry notes as typical of poetry produced by an oral-formulaic tradition.

Gardner, T. "How Free was the *Beowulf* Poet?" *MP* 71 (1973): 111-27. Argues that the *Beowulf* poet was not a prisoner of the oral-formulaic tradition but concentrated on words rather than formulas.

Greenfield, S. B. "The Canons of Old English Criticism." *ELH* 34 (1967):141-55. Attacks assumptions of the oral-formulaic school and argues that we need not reject the ordinary canon of literary judgment.

Heusler, Andreas. *Deutsche Versgeschichte mit Einschluss des altenglischen und altnordischen Stabreimverses.* 2 vols. Berlin and Leipzig: de Gruyter, 1925-29; reprint, 1956. The first important musical analysis of Old English prosody, assuming isochronous construction.

Isaacs, N. D. *Structural Principles of Old English Poetry.* Knoxville, Tenn.: University of Tennessee Press, 1968. Although not specifically concerned with *Beowulf,* Isaacs gives illuminating analyses of the Old English poet's art.

Kaluza, Max. *Englische Metrik in historischer Entwicklung dargestellt.* Berlin: E. Felber, 1909. Translated by A. C. Dunstan, under the title *A Short History of English Versification from the Earliest Time to the Present Day.* London: G. Allen & Co., 1911. Expands Sievers's types to ninety.

Lord, Alfred B. *The Singer of Tales.* Cambridge, Mass.: Harvard University Press, 1960; reprint, New York: Athenaeum, 1965. The standard introduction to the oral-formulaic theory of composition.

Luecke, Jane-Marie. *Measuring Old English Rhythm: An Application of the Principles of Gregorian Chant Rhythm to the*

Meter of "Beowulf." Madison: University of Wisconsin Press, 1978.

Magoun, F. P., Jr. "*Beowulf A'*: A Folk-Variant." *Arv: Journal of Scandinavian Folklore* 14(1958):95-101. This and the next item below are statements of Magoun's theory of the discrete origins of parts of *Beowulf.*

———. "*Beowulf B:* A Folk-Poem on Beowulf's Death." In A. Brown and P. Foote, eds. *Early English and Norse Studies Presented to Hugh Smith.* London: Methuen, 1963, pp. 127-40. See item above.

———. "The Oral-Formulaic Character of Anglo-Saxon Poetry." *Speculum* 28 (1953):446-67. Reprinted in *ABC, BP,* and *EA.* The seminal essay in the controversy about the oral-formulaic composition of *Beowulf.*

———. "The Theme of the Beasts of Battle in Anglo-Saxon Poetry." *NM* 56 (1955):81-90. A treatment of the formulaic theme of the raven, the wolf, and the eagle as accompaniment to Old English description of battle.

Nist, John. "Metrical Uses of the Harp in *Beowulf.*" In *OEP,* pp. 27-43.

Opland, Jeff. *Anglo-Saxon Oral Poetry: A Study of the Traditions.* New Haven, Conn.: Yale University Press, 1980. A survey of the evidence for the function of oral poetry in Anglo-Saxon society. Does not enter into formulaic or prosodic quarrels.

Parry, Milman. "Studies in the Epic Technique of Oral Verse-Making, I: Homer and the Homeric Style." *Harvard Studies in Classical Philology* 41 (1930):73-147. The study that provided the basis of the modern theory of oral-formulaic composition.

Peters, L. J. "The Relationship of the Old English *Andreas* to *Beowulf.*" *PMLA* 66 (1951):844-63. Rejection of the theory of "borrowing" between the two poems.

Pope, John C. *The Rhythm of Beowulf.* New Haven, Conn.: Yale University Press, 1942; reprint, 1966. The most influential statement of the isochronous theory of Anglo-Saxon verse rhythm.

Rogers, H. L. "The Crypto-Psychological Character of Oral Formula." *ES* 47 (1966):89-102. An attack on the theories of F. P. Magoun, Jr.

Sievers, Edouard. "Zur Rhythmik des germanisches Alliterationsverses I." *Beiträge zur Geschichte der Deutschen Sprache und Literatur* 10 (1885):209-314. The principal and most influential statement of Sievers's nonisochronous theory of Anglo-Saxon meter.

Stevick, R. D. "The Oral-Formulaic Analyses of Old English Verse." *Speculum* 37 (1962):382-89. Reprinted in *EA* and *OEL.* Discusses the ambiguities in the terminology used by followers of F. P. Magoun, Jr.

———. *Suprasegmentals, Meter, and the Manuscript of Beowulf.* The Hague: Mouton, 1968. Argues that the practice of the two manuscript scribes in spacing letters reveals that the metrical basis of *Beowulf* was rhythmic rather than syllabic and that it was probably isochronous, as maintained by John C. Pope.

Taglicht, J. "*Beowulf* and Old English Verse Rhythm." *RES* n.s., 12 (1961):341-51. An attack on both Edouard Sievers and John C. Pope that proposes instead a classical prosody for Anglo-Saxon poetry.

Watts, Ann C. *The Lyre and the Harp: A Comparative Reconsideration of Oral Tradition in Homer and Old English Epic Poetry.* New Haven, Conn.: Yale University Press, 1969. A survey of the history of the oral-formulaic theory and an examination of its shortcomings as applied to Old English poetry.

Whallon, William. "The Diction of *Beowulf*." *PMLA* 76 (1961): 309-19. Stresses the *Beowulf* poet's powers of variation and the appropriateness of epithet to context.

———. *Formula, Character, and Context: Studies in Homeric, Old English, and Old Testament Poetry.* Publication of Center for Hellenic Studies, Washington D.C. Cambridge, Mass.: Harvard University Press, 1969. An impressive study of formulaic composition as it relates to several issues, including the Christianity of *Beowulf.* Emphasizes the differences in method between Homer and the *Beowulf* poet. Incorporates Whallon's earlier articles.

———. "The Idea of God in *Beowulf.*" *PMLA* 80 (1965):19-23. Holds that the idea of God was determined partly by the traditional Germanic formulas—that *Beowulf* "never had anything to do with Christ until recently" (p. 22).

General Literary Criticism

Anderson, G. K. *The Literature of the Anglo-Saxons.* Princeton, N.J.: Princeton University Press, 1949. A survey that has been strongly criticized by specialist scholars but is useful for the overall picture.

Barnes, D. R. "Folktale Morphology and the Structure of *Beowulf.*" *Speculum* 45 (1970):416-34. Finds that Vladimir Propp's theory of the folktale's morphology is valid in describing the structure of *Beowulf.*

Batchelor, C. C. "The Style of the *Beowulf.*" *Speculum* 12 (1937): 330-42. An early and important purely literary study of *Beowulf.*

Benson, Larry D. "The Pagan Coloring of *Beowulf.*" In *OEP,* pp. 193-213. An interesting and unorthodox suggestion that the pagan, not the Christian, elements were "added" by the poet.

Bessinger, Jess B., Jr., and Stanley J. Kahrl, eds. *Essential Articles for the Study of Old English Poetry.* Hamden, Conn.: Archon Books, 1968. The most comprehensive of all the collections of scholarly and critical pieces, with great emphasis upon *Beowulf.* Abbreviated *EA.*

Blackburn, F. A. "The Christian Coloring in the *Beowulf.*" *PMLA* 12 (1897):205-25. Reprinted in *ABC.* Formulates what is now called the monkish-interpolation theory.

Blomfield, J. "The Style and Structure of *Beowulf.*" *RES,* o.s., 14 (1938):396-403. Reprinted in *BP.* Argues a formal unity and no progression in *Beowulf.*

Bloomfield, Morton W. "*Beowulf* and Christian Allegory: An Interpretation of Unferth." *Traditio* 7 (1949-51):410-15. Reprinted in *ABC*. Seizes upon Unferth's all-too-suggestive name and his function to see him as an essentially allegorical character.

Bonjour, Adrian. *The Digressions in Beowulf. Medium Ævum Monographs,* vol. 5. Oxford: B. H. Blackwell, 1950; reprint, 1965. A genial and intelligent discussion of those elements of the poem that most disquiet modern readers.

———. *Twelve Beowulf Papers, 1940-1960.* Geneva: Librairie E. Droz, 1962. A collection of Bonjour's most valuable work.

Brodeur, Arthur G. *The Art of Beowulf.* Berkeley, Calif.: University of California Press, 1959; reprint, 1969. The most useful general work of criticism.

Campbell, Alistair. "The Use in *Beowulf* of Earlier Heroic Verse." In Peter Clemoes and Kathleen Hughes, eds. *England Before the Conquest: Studies in Primary Sources Presented to Dorothy Whitelock.* Cambridge: Cambridge University Press, 1971, pp. 283-92. A good brief summary, in light of modern theory of *Beowulf*'s composition, of earlier heroic sources.

Creed, Robert P., ed. *Old English Poetry: Fifteen Essays.* Providence, R.I.: Brown University Press, 1967. About half the essays deal with *Beowulf,* with some emphasis upon prosody and the use of the harp. Abbreviated *OEP.*

Donahue, Charles. "*Beowulf* and the Christian Tradition: A Reconsideration from a Celtic Stance." *Traditio* 21 (1965):55-116. Concludes that Beowulf is not allegorically Christ but conveys a suggestion of him.

DuBois, A. E. "The Unity of *Beowulf.*" *PMLA* 49 (1934):374-405. Shows that the poem draws its unity from both historical background and philosophy and is for its age the "highly cultured equivalent of drama" (p. 405).

Eliason, N. E. "The Burning of Heorot." *Speculum* 55 (1980): 75-83. Discusses the destruction of Heorot as a device for a structured anticipation.

Gang, T. M. "Approaches to *Beowulf.*" *RES,* n.s., 3 (1952):1-12. An attack on Tolkien's imaginative criticism of *Beowulf.*

Gardner, J. *The Construction of Christian Poetry in Old English.*

Carbondale, Ill.: Southern Illinois University Press, 1975. An interesting, nonextremist study of the Christian poetic element.

Goldsmith, M. E. *The Mode and Meaning of Beowulf.* London: Athlone Press of the University of London, 1970. Supersedes her earlier articles on the Christian allegory of *Beowulf.*

Greenfield, S. B. *A Critical History of Old English Literature.* New York: New York University Press, 1965. A good survey, with an eclectic discussion of *Beowulf.*

――――. *The Interpretation of Old English Poems.* London: Routlege and Kegan Paul, 1972. An effort to describe the possibility for criticism of the poetry.

Hamilton, Marie P. "The Religious Principle in *Beowulf.*" *PMLA* 61 (1946):309-31. Reprinted in *ABC.* A palatable statement of the Christian content of the poem.

Irving, Edward B., Jr. *A Reading of Beowulf.* New Haven, Conn.: Yale University Press, 1968. An excellent discussion of style and structure.

Kahrl, S. J. "Feuds in *Beowulf:* A Tragic Necessity." *MP* 69 (1972):189-98. Suggests that the repetition of the feud theme in the poem is a way of indicating that, though the northern peoples might be saved from the supernatural by Beowulf, they can never be saved from themselves.

Kaske, R. E. "*Sapientia et Fortitudo* as the Controlling Theme of *Beowulf.*" *SP* 55 (1958):423-57. Reprinted in *ABC.* A strong argument for some levels of allegorical intent in the poem.

Lee, A. A. *The Guest-Hall of Eden.* New Haven, Conn.: Yale University Press, 1972. Argues that "*Beowulf* is a poem about hell's possession of middle-earth" (p. 171). A stimulating interpretation of motifs.

Leyerle, John. "Beowulf the Hero and the King." *MÆ* 34 (1965): 89-102. Suggests that the fatal contradiction in heroic society is reflected in *Beowulf.* Society requires a king who acts for the common good, whereas the heroic code exalts the individual.

――――. "The Interlace Structure of *Beowulf.*" *UTQ* 36 (1967):

1-17. A stimulating discussion of the relation of ornamental style in Anglo-Saxon arts to the composition of *Beowulf.*

Lumiansky, R. M. "The Dramatic Audience of *Beowulf.*" *JEGP* 51 (1952):545-50. Reprinted in *BP.* Suspense is maintained by the poet's use of the characters of the poem who view the action and respond to it.

McGalliard, J. C. "The Poet's Comments in *Beowulf,*" *SP,* 75 (1978), 243-70. Contrasts the poet's grim anticipations with the hero's confident hopes.

McNamee, Maurice B., S.J. "*Beowulf*—An Allegory of Salvation?" *JEGP* 59 (1960):190-207. Reprinted in *ABC.* The answer to the question in the title is yes.

Malone, Kemp. "*Beowulf.*" *ES* 29 (1948):161-72. Reprinted in *ABC.* Discusses the poet's use of digressions to illuminate themes of the poem, particularly those of Germanic patriotism.

————. *The Old English Period to 1100: A Literary History of England.* Edited by Albert C. Baugh. New York: Appleton-Century-Crofts, 1948. The standard survey covering most aspects of Old English literature.

Mitchell, B. "'Until the Dragon Comes . . .': Some Thoughts on *Beowulf,*" *Neophil* 47 (1963):126-38. Opposes the excesses of the Christian allegorists.

Moorman, Charles. "The Essential Paganism of *Beowulf.*" *MLQ* 28 (1967):3-18. A stubborn but appealing attempt to read *Beowulf* as primarily a heroic, non-Christian statement.

Nicholson, Lewis E. "The Literal Meaning and Symbolic Structure of *Beowulf.*" *C&M* 25 (1964):151-201. An example of the more extreme Christian-allegorical positions.

————, ed. *An Anthology of Beowulf Criticism.* Notre Dame, Ind.: University of Notre Dame Press, 1963. The earliest collection of standard pieces of criticism, with some bias toward the Christian view of *Beowulf.* Abbreviated *ABC.*

Niles, J. D. "Ring Composition and the Structure of *Beowulf.*" *PMLA* 94 (1979):924-35. Argues that the poem is constructed in sections by a concentric "ring" method, building outward concentrically from an interior "kernel."

O'Loughlin, J. L. N. "*Beowulf*—Its Unity and Purpose." *MÆ*

21 (1952):1-13. Maintains that the Germanic ethic and the Christian are closely related in the poem.

Osborn, M. "The Great Feud: Scriptural History and Strife in *Beowulf.*" *PMLA* 93 (1978):973-81. Argues that the poet parallels the pagan heroic world of the narrative with a cosmic Christian world by assigning a scriptural history to the monsters that Beowulf fights.

Pirkhofer, A. *Figurengestaltung im Beowulf-Epos. Anglistische Forschungen,* vol. 87 (Heidelberg, 1940). Analyzes the warrior ideal and the king ideal as represented in Wiglaf, Hrothgar, and Beowulf.

Raw, B. C. *The Art and Background of Old English Poetry.* London: E. Arnold, 1978. An excellent general introduction.

Rogers, H. L. "Beowulf's Three Great Fights." *RES,* n.s., 6 (1955): 339-55. Reprinted in *ABC.* Argues that the three fights are a progressive deterioration and that that does not allow the balanced structure assumed by many critics.

Rosier, James O. "Design for Treachery: The Unferth Intrigue." *PMLA* 76 (1962): 1-7. The ultimate in sophistication.

Schücking, L. L. "*Das Königsideal im Beowulf.*" *MHRA Bulletin* 3 (1929):143-54. Reprinted in translation, in *ABC.* An impressive statement of the Christian orientation of the theme of the ideal king.

Shippey, T. A. *Old English Verse.* London: Hutchinson University Library, 1972. A sound, skeptical survey of the literary problems of reading Old English poetry.

Sisam, Kenneth. *The Structure of Beowulf.* Oxford: Oxford University Press, 1965. A stimulating attack on all who like to think of *Beowulf* as a poem in any modern sense.

Stevick, R. D. "Christian Elements and the Genesis of *Beowulf.*" *MP* 61 (1963):79-89. Attempts to relate the formulaic nature of the poem to its Christian elements.

Stevens, Martin. "The Structure of *Beowulf:* From Gold-Hoard to Word-Hoard." *MLQ* 39 (1978):219-38. Writes that the poem's unity lies as much in poetic texture as in narrative.

———, and Jerome Mandel, eds. *Old English Literature.* Lincoln, Nebr.: University of Nebraska Press, 1968. Although only three of the essays are on *Beowulf* specifically, nearly all touch on the poem. Gives a useful selection of points of view. Abbreviated *OEL.*

Timmer, B. J. "*Beowulf:* The Poem and Its Poet." *Neophil* 32 (1948):122-26. Sees the poem as a compromise between pagan and Christian elements.

Tolkien, J. R. R. "*Beowulf:* The Monsters and the Critics." *PBA* 22 (1936):245-95. This famous paper was originally the Sir Israel Gollancz Memorial Lecture of 1936, and it has been reprinted as a pamphlet by the British Academy. London: Oxford University Press, 1958; reprint, 1960, etc. Also reprinted in *ABC* and *BP.*

————. "Prefatory Remarks." In J. R. Clark Hall, trans. *Beowulf and the Finnsburg Fragment.* Rev. ed., with intro. and notes by C. L. Wrenn. London: G. Allen and Unwin, 1950, pp. ix-xlii. Tolkien's remarks on the structure of Old English poetry are among the most helpful.

Van Meurs, J. C. "*Beowulf* and Literary Criticism." *Neophil* 39 (1955):114-30. Rejects Tolkien's symbolic interpretation.

Weil, Simone. *The* Iliad, *or the Poem of Force.* Wallingford, Pa.: Pendle Hill, 1956.

Wrenn, Charles L. *A Study of Old English Literature.* London: G. C. Harrap, 1967. A solid historical and critical survey.

Wright, H. G. "Good and Evil; Light and Darkness; Joy and Sorrow in *Beowulf.*" *RES,* n.s., 8 (1957):1-11. Reprinted in *ABC.* Deals with the balance of themes in the structure of the poem.

212

Index

A

Abraham, as a type of Beowulf: 176
Achilles: 50, 90
Ælfric: 32, 187n.
Aeneid: 24
Æschere: 60, 61, 140
Aesir: 51
Aidan, Saint: 19
Ajax: 50
Alchfrid: 24
Alcinous: 50
Alcuin: 8, 9, 23, 187n.
Aldfrid: 18, 24, 25
Aldhelm: 9, 19, 23, 25
Alexander: 3, 171
Alfred the Great: 20, 23, 33-39, 97, 101, 187n.
Allegorical interpretation of *Beowulf:* 170-77
Alliteration: *see* versification
Andreas: 12, 145, 146
Andrew, Saint: 10
Anglo-Saxon Chronicle, The: 97
Antaeus: 90
Aristotle: 3, 171
Arthur, King: 44

Ashburnham House: 4
Asser *(Life of Alfred):* 9
Authorship of *Beowulf:* 20-26, 179
Avalon: 44

B

Balder: 89
Barrow, Beowulf's: 85
Batchelor, C. C.: 160.
Battle of Brunnanburh: 8, 11, 148
Battle of Maldon (Byrtnoths Tod): 5, 8, 11, 37, 97, 106, 108, 190n.
Baum, Paull F.: 115, 121-22, 127, 128, 191n.; *see also* versification
Beasts of battle (theme): 107, 148-49
Beau(w): 89
Bede, the Venerable: 8, 9, 18, 23, 24, 73, 88, 97, 101, 190n.
Benedict Biscop: 26